THE NATIVE CONQUISTADOR

THE NATIVE CONQUISTADOR

Alva Ixtlilxochitl's Account of the Conquest of New Spain

**Edited and translated by
Amber Brian, Bradley Benton, and Pablo García Loaeza**

The Pennsylvania State University Press
University Park, Pennsylvania

Library of Congress Cataloging-in-Publication Data

Alva Ixtlilxochitl, Fernando de, 1578–1650, author.
The native conquistador : Alva Ixtlilxochitl's account
of the conquest of New Spain / edited and translated
by Amber Brian, Bradley Benton, and Pablo Garcia
Loaeza.
        pages   cm—(Latin American originals ; 10)
Summary: "An English translation of Alva Ixtlilxochitl's "Thirteenth Relation," an early seventeenth-
century narrative of the conquest of Mexico from
Hernando Cortés's arrival in 1519 through his
expedition into Central America in 1524"—Provided
by publisher.
Includes bibliographical references and index.
ISBN 978-0-271-06685-1 (pbk. : alk. paper)
1. Mexico—History—Conquest, 1519–1540.
2. Ixtlixochitl, Hernando, 1500–1531.
3. Cortés, Hernán, 1485–1547.
4. Indians of Mexico—History—16th century.
I. Brian, Amber, 1970– , editor, translator.
II. Benton, Bradley, 1980– , editor, translator.
III. Loaeza, Pablo García, 1972– , editor, translator.
IV. Title. V. Series: Latin American originals ; 10.

F1230.A46 2015
972'.02—dc23
2015003562

CONTENTS

ILLUSTRATIONS

Figures

Maps

Latin American Originals (LAO) is a series of primary source texts on colonial Latin America. LAO volumes are accessible, affordable editions of texts translated into English—most of them for the very first time. Of the ten volumes now in print, seven illuminate aspects of the Spanish conquests during the long century of 1494 to 1614, and three push our understandings of the spiritual conquest into surprising new territories.

Taken in the chronological order of their primary texts, *Of Cannibals and Kings* (LAO 7) comes first. It presents the earliest written attempts to describe the native cultures of the Americas, offering striking insight into how the first Europeans in the Americas struggled from the very start to conceive a New World.

This newest volume in the series, *The Native Conquistador* (LAO 10), comes next, as its primary source tells the story of the famous Spanish conquest expeditions into Mexico and Central America from 1519 to 1524. But this is far from being a repeat of the well-known narrative of Cortés's exploits, giving us instead an indigenous perspective, built around an alternative leading protagonist (Ixtlilxochitl, the king of Tetzcoco), written by his great-great-grandson. Viewed through the prism of the Ixtlilxochitl dynasty, the conquest of Mexico looks very different—and will never be quite the same again.

Next, chronologically, are LAO 2, 1, and 9. *Invading Guatemala* shows how reading multiple accounts of conquest wars (in this case, Spanish, Nahua, and Maya versions of the Guatemalan conflict of the 1520s) can explode established narratives and suggest a more complex and revealing conquest story. *Invading Colombia* challenges us to view the difficult Spanish invasion of Colombia in the 1530s as more representative of conquest campaigns than the better-known assaults on the Aztec and Inca Empires. It complements

The Improbable Conquest, which presents letters written between 1537 and 1556 by Spaniards struggling to found a colony along the hopefully named Río de la Plata. Their trials and tribulations make the persistence of the colonists seem improbable indeed.

The Conquest on Trial (LAO 3) features a fictional embassy of Native Americans filing a complaint over the conquest in a court in Spain—the Court of Death. That text, the first theatrical examination of the conquest published in Spain, effectively condensed contemporary debates on colonization into one dramatic package. It contrasts well with *Defending the Conquest* (LAO 4), which presents a spirited, ill-humored, and polemic apologia for the Spanish conquest, written in 1613 by a lesser-known veteran conquistador.

LAO volumes 5, 6, and 8 all explore aspects of Spanish efforts to implant Christianity in the New World. *Forgotten Franciscans* casts new light on the spiritual conquest and the conflictive cultural world of the Inquisition in sixteenth-century Mexico. *Gods of the Andes* presents the first English edition of a 1594 manuscript describing Inca religion and the campaign to convert native Andeans. Its Jesuit author is surprisingly sympathetic to preconquest beliefs and practices, viewing them as preparing Andeans for the arrival of the faith he helped bring from Spain. Both LAO 5 and 6 expose wildly divergent views within the church in Spanish America—both on native religions and on how to replace them with Christianity. Complementing those two volumes by revealing the indigenous side to the same process, *Translated Christianities* presents religious texts translated from Nahuatl and Yucatec Maya. Designed to proselytize and ensure the piety of indigenous parishioners, these texts show how such efforts actually contributed to the development of local Christianities. As in other parts of the Americas, native cultures thrived within the conversion process, leading to fascinatingly multifaceted outcomes.

The source texts to LAO volumes are either colonial-era rare books or archival documents—written in European languages or in indigenous ones such as Nahuatl and Maya. The contributing authors are historians, anthropologists, and scholars of literature; they have developed a specialized knowledge that allows them to locate, translate, and present these texts in a way that contributes to scholars' understanding of the period, while also making them readable for students and nonspecialists. Amber Brian, Bradley Benton, and two-time LAO author Pablo García are just such scholars, allowing them to create this fascinating and important contribution to the series and to the New Conquest History.

—Matthew Restall

Written in Spanish at the beginning of the seventeenth century, don Fernando de Alva Ixtlilxochitl's "Thirteenth Relation" of his *Compendio histórico del reino de Texcoco* [Historical Compendium of the Kingdom of Tetzcoco] addresses the history of the conquest of New Spain from Hernando Cortés's arrival in Yucatan in 1519 through his expedition into Central America in 1524. The central protagonist of the story, however, is not the Spanish conquistador but Alva Ixtlilxochitl's great-great-grandfather, the native prince Ixtlilxochitl of Tetzcoco, who was in this account a quick convert to Christianity and "whose aid in winning [Mexico] was second only to God's."

Our title, *The Native Conquistador*, deliberately calls to mind Matthew Restall's *Maya Conquistador* (1998) and Laura Matthew and Michel Oudijk's edited volume, *Indian Conquistadors: Indigenous Allies in the Conquest of Mesoamerica* (2007). These two groundbreaking studies represent a trend in scholarship on the conquest period that is commonly referred to as "New Conquest History." One of its central features has been the reassessment of the roles of native Mesoamericans, both as protagonists in conquest campaigns and as chroniclers of those events (Restall 2012). *The Native Conquistador*, which highlights the role of Ixtlilxochitl, offers Alva Ixtlilxochitl's perspective on the events of the conquest and complicates and enriches the standard narrative. In particular, the text reveals the complex political dynamics that motivated Tetzcoco's alliance with Cortés. At the same time, it exposes tensions and contradictions that speak to the complexity of indigenous identity in colonial Mexico during the century after the conquest. There is no translation of the text currently in circulation; this book aims to fill that void.

We thank Matthew Restall for his early interest in this project and for his encouragement throughout its development. The editorial and production staff at Penn State Press has been superb at every stage. We are also thankful to the external reviewers, whose comments helped us to refine our work, and to Susan Silver, who exercised her duties as copyeditor with tremendous care. We are indebted to the Obermann Center for Advanced Studies at the University of Iowa, which afforded us the necessary space and strategic support to undertake the first draft of the translation through an Interdisciplinary Research Grant in the summer of 2013. The collaborative working environment was essential to our project's progress, while the enthusiasm and curiosity of our fellow inhabitants of the Obermann house, particularly its director, Teresa Mangum, and assistant director, Jennifer New, heartened our work. We would also like to thank Susan Schroeder and Stafford Poole for their insights into the complexities of Chimalpahin and early modern Catholicism, respectively.

ABBREVIATIONS

AGN   Archivo General de la Nación, Mexico City
    -I   Indios
    -Inq   Inquisición
    -IV   Indiferente Virreinal
    -T   Tierras
    -V   Vínculos

CC INAH   Códice Chimalpahin, Instituto Nacional de Antropología e Historia, Mexico City

Introduction

Tetzcoco's Native Conquistadors

In the autumn of 1520 Hernando Cortés and his men prepared for a second invasion of Mexico-Tenochtitlan, the capital city of the Triple Alliance (often called the Aztec Empire). Their first attempt, begun a year earlier, had ended badly; in late June 1520 they were forced to flee the city after dark and sustained heavy casualties in what was later called the *noche triste*, or sad night. By December 1520, however, they were better prepared. They had spent the intervening year licking their wounds and formulating a two-pronged battle plan in which they would attack by boat and by marching along the three causeways linking the island city to the mainland. And, more important, they had attracted a large contingent of indigenous allies from across the region. These indigenous fighters were crucial to the Spaniards' eventual victory.

The most famous of Cortés's native allies were those from the Nahua *altepetl*, or city-state, of Tlaxcala, which remained independent of the Triple Alliance at the time of the Spanish arrival.[1]

1. When referring to the inhabitants of central Mexico, we have chosen to use the term "Nahua," because they were speakers of the Nahuatl language. Though commonly referred to as Aztecs, Nahua groups at the time of conquest did not use that term; see Barlow (1945). Instead, native peoples were generally identified by the names of their altepetl. For example, inhabitants of Mexico-Tenochtitlan were called either Mexica or Tenochca. Whenever possible, we use these local names of the various Nahua groups, such as the Tlaxcalteca or the Tetzcoca. For the dominant political structure in place in central Mexico at the time of conquest, we use the term "Triple Alliance"; see Carrasco (1999).

The alliance of Tetzcoco, Mexico-Tenochtitlan, and Tlacopan had jointly gained dominance over vast swaths of Mesoamerica. The Tlaxcalteca, as the traditional enemies of this Triple Alliance, were persuaded to join Cortés's cause fairly easily. But Cortés was also able to attract fighters from the city of Tetzcoco, a founding member of the Triple Alliance and traditionally one of Mexico-Tenochtitlan's staunchest supporters. Reflecting the factionalism of Nahua politics, the Tetzcoca who chose to fight alongside the Spaniards betrayed their own federation. The version of the conquest presented here, written by don Fernando de Alva Ixtlilxochitl, represents the perspective of the Tetzcoca who supported the Spaniards and emphasizes the role of the author's ancestor, Ixtlilxochitl, who appears at Cortés's side throughout the conquest of New Spain. Alva Ixtlilxochitl laments, however, that "Cortés did not mention Ixtlilxochitl or his exploits or heroic deeds," and he worked steadily to remedy that omission with his account.

Not everyone in Tetzcoco was eager to join the Spaniards. The Tetzcoca ruler Coanacoch, for instance, fled to Tenochtitlan as the Spaniards approached. But several of Coanacoch's brothers and half brothers sided with the Spaniards. According to the account of the conquest campaigns that Cortés presented in his October 30, 1520, letter to Emperor Charles V, one of Coanacoch's younger half brothers, don Fernando Tecocoltzin, "bore a great love for the Spaniards," and Cortés installed him as ruler in Tetzcoco after Coanacoch's departure. Cortés wrote that to return the favor, Tecocoltzin "did all he could to persuade his vassals to come and fight against Temixtitan [sic, Tenochtitlan] and expose themselves to the same danger and hardships as ourselves. He spoke with his brothers . . . and entreated them to go to my assistance with all the people in their domains" (Cortés 1986, 220). The Tetzcoca ruling family, therefore, was divided, with some members fighting against the Spaniards and some fighting with them.[2] Cortés himself was aware of the complexity of the situation and the psychological effects of such a division. He asked King Charles to "imagine how valuable this help and friendship of Don Fernando was to me, and what the people of Temixtitan [sic, Tenochtitlan] must have felt on seeing advance against them those

---

2. Cortés was, in fact, exploiting existing divisions within the family. See Hicks (1994) and Townsend (2014b).

whom they held as vassals and friends, relatives and brothers, even fathers and sons" (221). The support from Tetzcoco was clearly important to the Spanish victory. One of the Spaniards fighting with Cortés, Bernal Díaz del Castillo, confirmed the importance of Tetzcoca support. "Don Hernando [Tecocoltzin]," wrote Díaz del Castillo, "offered all the assistance within his power, and of his own accord promised to send messengers to all the neighbouring pueblos and tell them to become vassals of His Majesty, and accept our friendship and authority against Mexico[-Tenochtitlan]" (2009, 243). Without Tecocoltzin's support, Tetzcoco and the surrounding region might not have been as sympathetic to the Spanish cause. And had the Triple Alliance remained unified, the Spaniards would have had a more difficult time bringing central Mexico under their control. Such a small group of Europeans could hardly have subdued the region's large population if all the native peoples had been united in their resistance to the invaders; exploiting fissures within the indigenous political landscape and winning over indigenous supporters was crucial to Cortés's success. Native allies made the Spanish conquest of Mexico possible. The diverse attitudes of the Tetzcoca toward the Spaniards were emblematic of the larger trend in Mesoamerica: some native people resisted Spanish conquest while others participated as conquerors themselves.

For many years scholars of the conquest worked to shift focus away from the Spanish perspective and bring attention to the often-ignored voices and viewpoints of the Indians and to emphasize what some referred to as the "vision of the vanquished."[3] But recent work

3. The phrase "vision of the vanquished" is drawn from León-Portilla's *Visión de los vencidos*, originally published in 1959 and now in its twenty-ninth edition. The volume presents a compilation of native sources woven into a unified narrative, and for decades it has been a mainstay of primary-text reading related to the conquest of Mexico, both in Spanish and in English translation as *The Broken Spears*, first published in 1962. *Visión de los vencidos* marks a shift away from Spanish perspectives on the conquest in mid-twentieth-century scholarship, but by no means is it the sole example. For studies that explore the native perspective and are based on Spanish-language sources, Gibson (1952, 1964) was especially transformative. See also Gerhard (1972), Taylor (1972), Farriss (1984), Clendinnen (1987), and Gruzinski (1988). Studies based on native-language texts began to appear at roughly the same time and have increased in frequency in the past few decades. See Anderson and Dibble (1950–82), León-Portilla (1956), Anderson, Berdan, and Lockhart (1976), Lockhart (1992), Kellogg (1995), Restall (1997), and Terraciano (2001). While all these studies focus squarely on native perspectives, they differ in the degree to which they emphasize native defeat

that highlights the "Indian conquistadors" has forced scholars to reexamine the simple categories of conqueror and subject, or aggressor and victim, and to acknowledge the seemingly contradictory roles and complex position of native peoples who chose to fight other native groups alongside the Spaniards.[4] This work has demonstrated that the Spaniards relied on native allies in their subjugation of Tenochtitlan and in the later campaigns into the northern and southern reaches of Mesoamerica and that, at times, native peoples even undertook conquests independently of the Spaniards.[5] Alva Ixtlilxochitl's "Thirteenth Relation: On the Arrival of the Spaniards and the Beginning of the Law of the Gospel" falls within the scope of this recent trend in studies of the conquest.[6] It exposes the complex political reality that moved some of Tetzcoco's leaders to join the Spaniards against the Mexica. The text also reveals that, in spite of the upheavals wrought by conquest and colonization, ethnic identities endured, as did partisan allegiances—in this case, to Tetzcoco and its erstwhile ruling dynasty. These loyalties were deeply bound up with ways of remembering and recording the past.

Alva Ixtlilxochitl wrote his "Thirteenth Relation" nearly a century after the conclusion of the conquest battles in Mexico-Tenochtitlan. In his telling of the story, Cortés's success hinged on his alliance with Tetzcoco and, even more important, on his personal friendship with

---

and cultural loss on the one hand and native resiliency, accommodation, and negotiation on the other.

4. The idea of Indian-as-conquistador is one of the hallmarks of a body of scholarship that has come to be known as the "New Conquest History." One of the goals of this school is to identify what Restall (2012, 155) has called "new protagonists" of the conquest. Representative works have come from a variety of disciplines, including history (e.g., Horn 1997; Restall 1998; Sousa and Terraciano 2003; Wood 2003; Restall and Asselbergs 2007; Schroeder 2010b; Schroeder et al. 2010; Yannakakis 2011; Matthew 2012), anthropology (e.g., Burkhart 1989; Oudijk 2000; Hassig 2006; Tavárez 2011), art history (e.g., Peterson 1993; Mundy 1996; Boone 2000; Asselbergs 2008; Diel 2008; Leibsohn 2009), and literature (e.g., Adorno 2007). For an overview of New Conquest History, see Restall (2012).

5. On the role of Nahua allies in conquests outside central Mexico, see, for instance, Restall and Asselbergs (2007), Asselbergs (2008), Altman (2010), Matthew (2012), and McEnroe (2014).

6. The ongoing search for alternative perspectives on the conquest and colonization of America has led to an increased interest in the work of Alva Ixtlilxochitl. Some recent insights appear in a special issue of the *Colonial Latin American Review*; see Benton (2014), Brian (2014b), García Loaeza (2014a), Kauffman (2014), Townsend (2014a), and Villella (2014).

Alva Ixtlilxochitl's great-great-grandfather: don Fernando Cortés Ixtlilxochitl. This is one of the defining features of Alva Ixtlilxochitl's version of the conquest, which consistently presents Ixtlilxochitl as the most important of Cortés's indigenous allies. Ixtlilxochitl was, according to Alva Ixtlilxochitl, "the greatest and most loyal ally [Cortés] had in this land and whose aid in winning this land was second only to God's."

Featuring Ixtlilxochitl prominently throughout the text, the "Thirteenth Relation" begins with the arrival of the Spaniards off the gulf coast of Mexico in 1519. The narrative then moves quickly through the well-known episodes of the conquest—Moteucçoma's (also spelled Montezuma or Moctezuma) imprisonment, Narváez's frustrated attempt to subdue Cortés, the Toxcatl festival and massacre, and the *noche triste* debacle. The pace slows considerably as Alva Ixtlilxochitl describes the second campaign to conquer Tenochtitlan. Nonetheless, the final surrender of Cuauhtemoc and fall of Tenochtitlan occur before the halfway point in the text. The remainder of the account is dedicated to several expeditions conducted outside of central Mexico.

The Spanish conquests in the New World were organized in relay fashion, whereby newly conquered areas served as staging grounds for further exploration and conquest.[7] The expedition led by Cortés, for instance, arrived from Cuba, whose first European settlement had been established only a few years earlier, in 1511. Similarly, once Mexico-Tenochtitlan had been conquered, the Spaniards fanned out in all directions looking for other places to conquer. In Alva Ixtlilxochitl's version, Ixtlilxochitl follows the Spaniards on these subsequent campaigns: to Pánuco in the northeast; to Michoacan and Colima in the west; and to Oaxaca, Tehuantepec, and Tabasco in southern Mexico. The "Thirteenth Relation" also includes a summary description of the conquest of Guatemala. The narrative then returns to central Mexico, to highlight the official introduction of the law of the Gospel by a group of distinguished Franciscan friars. The final third of the text is devoted to Cortés's infamous journey to Las Hibueras (spelled Yhueras in the manuscript) in modern Honduras, during which the deposed rulers of the Triple Alliance capitals, who were traveling with

7. For an explanation of the organization of conquest expeditions, see Lockhart and Schwartz (1983, 78–85).

Cortés as hostages, were hanged. As Alva Ixtlilxochitl dramatically portrays it, these kings were unjustly killed by a ruthless and conniving Cortés. Ixtlilxochitl was the only native leader to return alive. The text ends with news of the rebuilding of Mexico City, which in this account is spearheaded by the tireless Ixtlilxochitl.

Multiple Perspectives on the Conquest of Mexico

The primary-source narratives of the conquest of Mexico are remarkable for the variety of perspectives they offer. Cortés wrote extensively of his exploits in five letters to King Charles of Spain.[8] Cortés's reports were intended not merely to inform the monarch and people in Europe of the Spanish exploits in New Spain but also to justify his actions. Cortés was authorized not to engage in conquest in the interior but only to survey the coastal areas. By embarking on his campaign of conquest, he openly disregarded the orders of Diego Velázquez, the Cuban governor under whom he served. Consequently, his actions in Mexico constituted insubordination, if not treason. In that context, his accounts of the conquest of Mexico had the ulterior objective of bypassing Velázquez, whose authority he had spurned, to appeal directly to the king for his royal approval.[9] In his carefully crafted texts, Cortés represented himself as a loyal vassal and his conquest of Mexico as a great service to the Crown. His rhetorical strategies worked; he was not prosecuted for his insubordination but rather awarded several large *encomiendas*, or grants of indigenous labor and tribute, in Mexico along with the noble title Marquis of the Valley of Oaxaca.[10]

---

8. Of the five letters Cortés wrote to the king, the first was lost, the second and third were published in Seville in 1522 and 1523, and the fourth was published in Toledo in 1525. All three were quickly translated for publication in Latin, French, and Italian. The fifth and final letter from 1526 chronicles Cortés's expedition to Honduras and remained unpublished until the nineteenth century (Cortés 1986, lxxii–lxxviii). The first known document produced by the Spaniards in Mexico is a 1519 petition, only recently published, from the municipal council of the newly founded town of Veracruz. See Schwaller and Nader (2014).

9. See John H. Elliott's introductory essay, "Cortés, Velázquez, and Charles V," in Cortés (1986, xi–xxxvii).

10. Brading (1991, 26–28). On the life of Hernando Cortés, see Martínez (1990). For an appraisal of Cortés's narrative strategies, see Pastor Bodmer (1992).

Cortés was never completely satisfied with his situation, however. What he really wanted was to be named governor of this newly conquered territory of New Spain (a name first used by Cortés, in fact).[11] The king and his council, though, were wary of granting the conquistadors too much power and excluded Cortés from any influential government position. Fearing for the preservation of his fortune and his historical legacy, Cortés asked his chaplain, Francisco López de Gómara, to write a history of the conquest of Mexico based mainly on Cortés's own accounts. The resulting text, *Historia de la conquista de México*, would surely have pleased Cortés, had he lived to see it published in 1552, five years after his death. In it, Gómara heaps unrelenting praise on the conquistador, casting him as an epic hero in the Spaniards' quest to bring spiritual salvation and civilization to a pagan and barbaric people.[12]

Other Spaniards who had fought in the conquest war were unhappy—even angry—with Cortés's and Gómara's version of events, which suggested that Cortés had done most of the work himself. The best-known attempt to rectify alleged inaccuracies and exaggerations in those accounts is the *True History of the Conquest of New Spain*, written by Bernal Díaz del Castillo, who participated in the conquest battles of the 1520s and, by the 1550s, was increasingly frustrated by the lack of recognition and compensation that he and other conquistadors had received. Moreover, by the mid-sixteenth century, the Crown was trying to wrest control of the *encomiendas* from the aging conquistadors and prevent their children from inheriting them. Díaz del Castillo's history of the conquest was meant to secure economic stability for himself and his heirs, which he did by insisting that the conquest was the result of a collaborative effort and that he had made contributions worthy of compensation.[13] In Díaz del Castillo's account, the conquest was achieved through consensus decision making rather than as a result of Cortés's top-down, military-style leadership.

11. The viceroyalty of New Spain eventually came to include mainland North America from present-day California south into Central America, as well as islands in the Caribbean and the Pacific, including the Philippines. In this volume, however, we use the term "New Spain" in its earlier and more limited sense to mean present-day Mexico and the greater part of Central America.

12. On Gómara's historiographic efforts, see Roa-de-la-Carrera (2005).

13. On Díaz del Castillo's account and its significance in the discursive tradition of the colonial period, see Adorno (1997).

The *True History*, then, paints a somewhat different picture of the conquest war in Mexico and serves as a useful foil for the versions told by Cortés and Gómara. Their varied perspectives notwithstanding, however, the Cortés, Gómara, and Díaz del Castillo accounts are all characterized by Spanish triumphalism and heroics. Theirs are epic stories, whose Spanish protagonists regularly engage in larger-than-life, even miraculous acts of valor. And this triumphalist perspective is reflected in the English-language histories that brought renewed attention to the conquest in the nineteenth century and has continued to influence popular understandings and portrayals of conquest history ever since.[14]

Since the Spaniards, who had at least a common sense of purpose, could not agree on a history of the conquest campaigns, it should come as no surprise that the versions told by native peoples themselves vary considerably more.[15] The most widely read and studied account of the conquest from a native perspective is found in the Florentine Codex.[16] Written in the mid-sixteenth century by native noblemen from the altepetl of Tlatelolco under the auspices of the Franciscan friar Bernardino de Sahagún, the Florentine Codex addresses the cultural practices and history of the Nahuas in two-column, side-by-side Spanish and Nahuatl alphabetic texts and nearly two thousand drawings. The final book, Book 12, narrates events of the conquest from a native perspective, but one that is highly specific to its Tlatelolca origin. Built on the same small island, Tlatelolco was Tenochtitlan's sister city, and inhabitants of both settlements identified themselves as Mexica. Tlatelolco, however, had been conquered and subjugated by the Tenochca in the

14. William Prescott's *Conquest of Mexico* (1843) was particularly influential. See Restall (2003b), Roa-de-la-Carrera (2005), Schroeder (2007), Adorno (2011), and Restall and Fernández-Armesto (2012).

15. Indigenous versions of the conquest began to attract sustained scholarly interest only in the second half of the twentieth century, beginning with León-Portilla (1959) and continuing with Lockhart (1993). Lockhart's *We People Here* provides annotated translations of six Nahuatl texts, including Book 12 of the Florentine Codex. Lockhart's methodology of carefully translating and analyzing indigenous-language texts for the study of colonial history became known as the "New Philology." See Restall (2003a).

16. The Florentine Codex was officially titled *Historia general de las cosas de Nueva España* (*General History of the Things of New Spain*). In addition to the studies by León-Portilla (1959) and Lockhart (1993) mentioned earlier, see Anderson and Dibble (1950–82), Martínez (1982), Terraciano (2010), and Wolf and Connors (2012).

1470s. The Tlatelolca point of view in Book 12 is unmistakable. The authors emphasize the bravery of the warriors from Tlatelolco while belittling the fighters from Tenochtitlan. Book 12 also portrays the Tenochca ruler Moteucçoma as incompetent and weak. The Tenochca version was not preserved in any known text, but it must have been very different.[17]

The highly local perspective that surfaces in Book 12 is a hallmark of indigenous texts generally, including Alva Ixtlilxochitl's. Individual or corporate authors wrote from the historical point of view of a particular altepetl and with specific interests in mind. This very circumscribed vantage point has sometimes been called "micropatriotic" in the central Mexican context (Lockhart 1993, 30). While the Tlatelolca wrote from the perspective of the defeated in the conquest war, they nonetheless managed to insert their disdain for the Tenochca into their account and built the case that they should be given at least as much recognition for their heroics as the Tenochca. Other altepetl, however, who had been faithful allies of the Spaniards offered versions of the conquest that varied significantly from the Mexica as they highlighted their contributions to the Spaniards' victory.

The Tlaxcalteca were renowned as the Spaniards' primary allies, and, unsurprisingly, histories produced in Tlaxcala emphasize their helpful role. The *Lienzo de Tlaxcala* is one such history, although the narrative appears in pictorial rather than alphabetic form.[18] Originally produced in the sixteenth century, the *Lienzo* highlights the assistance provided by the Tlaxcalteca and portrays them as conquistadors on the same order as the Spaniards, fighting together in scene after scene. The *Lienzo* clearly depicts the conquest of Mexico as a joint venture between Spaniards and Tlaxcalteca. Alphabetic texts from Tlaxcala tell a similar story. The *Historia de Tlaxcala* (1585) was written by Diego Muñoz Camargo, who as a mestizo historian is often compared with Alva Ixtlilxochitl. Unlike Alva Ixtlilxochitl, however, Muñoz Camargo emphasized the role of the Tlaxcalteca— not the Tetzcoca—as the Spaniards' indispensable allies in their

17. The sole surviving Mexica-Tenochca account of the Spanish conquest is the Codex Aubin. This text, however, is brief and fragmentary and not comparable to Book 12. See Lockhart (1993, 274–79).

18. The original sixteenth-century *lienzo*, or painting on cloth, is now lost. The images that survive are colonial-era copies made by native artists. See Asselbergs (2008, 232–35) and Kranz (2010).

efforts to conquer the Mexica. Moreover, Muñoz Camargo holds up the Tlaxcalteca ruler Maxixcatzin—not Tetzcoco's Ixtlilxochitl—as the single most important indigenous ally. Like most conquest narratives, this text also had a pragmatic purpose.[19] The *Historia* was presented along with other documents to King Philip II by the sixth Tlaxcalteca commission (1583–85) to draw attention to Tlaxcala's contribution to the conquest as its delegates petitioned for special privileges.[20]

Many other Nahua groups similarly sought to portray themselves as faithful Spanish allies and even to correct what they felt to be excessive acclaim given to the Tlaxcalteca. The town council of the altepetl of Huexotzinco, for example, sent a letter written in Nahuatl to King Philip II in 1560 stating that the Spaniards' most beneficial conquest-era alliance was the one they made with the Huexotzinca. They vehemently criticized the actions of the Tlaxcalteca, whom they felt to have been better compensated for their support of the Spaniards. The letter asserts that the Huexotzinca efforts in service of the Crown ought to have been remembered and rewarded with a reduced tax burden.[21] Native histories of the conquest, then, differ considerably. These versions were sometimes written with a specific monetary or other reward in mind and systematically underscore the decisive role played by a particular altepetl in the conquest campaigns.

In striking contrast, several native annals neglect to mention the Spanish arrival and conquest, or, if they do, they portray the foreign conquistadors as equivalent to other native conquering groups from the local past.[22] The Spaniards, particularly in the early years of the colony, acted very much like the Mexica had before them: they conquered by force of arms and then expected tribute payments but

19. Stephanie Merrim highlights the importance of "pragmatic context" for early colonial writings (1996, 61). Though she focuses on European-authored texts, her analysis can be extended to texts produced by indigenous authors.

20. Tlaxcala sent a series of delegations to Spain to obtain an audience with the king and secure privileges for the altepetl. The first delegation set out in 1527. The sixth and final commission, which included Muñoz Camargo, arrived in Spain in 1584 (Gibson 1952, 164–67).

21. For an introduction to the Huexotzinco letter and a translation of the letter itself, see Lockhart (1993).

22. Annals, the preferred genre of the native historian, were organized by year. In the precontact period, annals were pictorial documents; in the postconquest era, alphabetic versions quickly appeared alongside pictorial texts and continued to be produced long into the colonial period.

left many facets of everyday life untouched. The Spanish conquest was not a watershed event for many of the inhabitants of New Spain, especially if they had not been heavily involved in the conquest battles.[23] One annals text that minimizes the Spanish conquest was written in Nahuatl by don Domingo de San Antón Muñón Chimalpahin Quauhtlehuanitzin.[24] Chimalpahin has no entry for 1519, the year that the Spaniards arrived in central Mexico. And in the entries for the next two pivotal years of 1520 and 1521, when Cortés besieged and defeated Mexico-Tenochtitlan, Chimalpahin provides information that, while related to the conquest, does not explicitly address it. For 1520, for example, he says, "In this year the tlatoani Itzcahuatzin and Necuametzin died of smallpox" (1997, 1:425).[25] The text does not even hint that these deaths were a direct result of the conquest, since smallpox was introduced to the native population with the arrival of the Europeans. Chimalpahin's treatment of the Spanish conquest in this particular text suggests that he did not see it as an epic event in the same way that writers like Cortés, Díaz del Castillo, or the Tlaxcalteca did. Conquest was just something that happened in central Mexico, and the Spaniards were simply one more entry in the long list of conquerors in this region's history.

Chimalpahin's choice not to highlight the conquest does not imply that he was oblivious to it or disinterested in it. In fact, Chimalpahin rewrote Gómara's history of the conquest almost verbatim; he only interpolated some additional information related to native people.[26] Gómara's version of the conquest is also relevant to the "Thirteenth Relation," since it is clear that Alva Ixtlilxochitl borrowed heavily—at times nearly word for word—from Gómara's *Historia de la conquista de México*. Alva Ixtlilxochitl's reliance on this text is not altogether surprising as it provided a structural model and many details not to be found elsewhere. However, unlike Chimalpahin, who did not alter Gómara's history in a significant way, Alva Ixtlilxochitl

---

23. See Lockhart (1993, 6).

24. Many thanks to Susan Schroeder for directing us to this example. For more on the conquest as a "nonevent," see Schroeder (2007, 9–13).

25. Literally meaning "speaker," the Nahuatl term *tlatoani* (plural, *tlatoque*) refers to the ruler of an altepetl; Spaniards often equated this position with that of a European king.

26. Chimalpahin's purpose for rewriting the text is unclear; see Schroeder (2010a, 105).

revised the narrative to conform to his particular point of view. For Gómara, Cortés was the main protagonist, and only through Cortés's bravery, ingenuity, and skill was Mexico won. For Alva Ixtlilxochitl, on the other hand, the conquest of Mexico was the direct result of the sage guidance of his great-great-grandfather and namesake, Ixtlilxochitl of Tetzcoco, whose role in the success of the conquest was second in importance only to God's.

Alva Ixtlilxochitl and the "Thirteenth Relation"

Don Fernando de Alva Ixtlilxochitl was born in or around 1578, the second of nine children born to doña Ana Cortés Ixtlilxochitl and Juan Pérez de Peraleda.[27] His father was a Spaniard; his mother was a mestiza, the daughter of a Spaniard and an indigenous woman.[28] His mother was also the *cacica*, or native ruler (masculine: *cacique*), of San Juan Teotihuacan, an indigenous town located about fifteen miles to the north of Tetzcoco.[29] The title was linked to an entailed estate, a *cacicazgo*, which was the source of the family's wealth. The clan's prestige issued from its ties to the Tetzcoca ruling dynasty. Through his mother, Alva Ixtlilxochitl could trace his lineage back to Tetzcoco's famed precontact tlatoque Nezahualcoyotl (r. 1431–72) and Nezahualpilli (r. 1472–15), and to the conquest-era leader Ixtlilxochitl (fig. 1).[30]

While Alva Ixtlilxochitl's family was historically linked with Tetzcoco, their more immediate connections were with the town

---

27. Alva Ixtlilxochitl (1975–77, 2:341). One of Alva Ixtlilxochitl's younger brothers, Bartolomé de Alva, was a secular priest of the Catholic Church and is known among scholars today for his Nahuatl-language translations of Spanish Golden Age dramas and confessional texts; see Alva (1999) and Sell, Burkhart, and Wright (2008). For studies of the intellectual impact of both brothers, see Brian (2014a) and Schwaller (2014).

28. The right of Ana Cortés to her title and estate was legally challenged on the grounds that she was a Spaniard, not a native. See Alva Ixtlilxochitl (1975–77, 2:354–69).

29. During the classic period (ca. 1–900 C.E.), Teotihuacan was an important political and economic center, which is evidenced by the pyramid complex that remains today. That center was abandoned at the end of the classic period, however, and the postclassic- and colonial-era town known as Teotihuacan was a relatively small, obscure village and one of Tetzcoco's tributaries.

30. Ana Cortés Ixtlilxochitl's grandmother, also called Ana Cortés, was Ixtlilxochitl's daughter (AGN-V 232, fol. 16v).

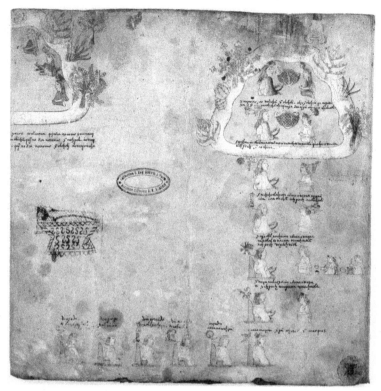

FIG. 1 The second panel of the Tlotzin Map, showing the hereditary rulers of Tetzcoco. Nezahualcoyotl and Nezahualpilli are represented on the column above Cacama, who ruled at the time of the Spaniards' arrival. The map was part of Alva Ixtlilxochitl's archive. Photo courtesy of and copyright by the Bibliothèque Nationale de France.

of Teotihuacan. However, and to complicate matters further, Alva Ixtlilxochitl's family had been living—at least part of the time—in Mexico City for two generations. Alva Ixtlilxochitl's maternal grandfather worked as an interpreter at the Audiencia (Spanish High Court) in Mexico City, as did Alva Ixtlilxochitl's father. Therefore, Alva Ixtlilxochitl's mother spent much of her life in New Spain's capital, and it is likely that Alva Ixtlilxochitl did as well.[31] Nevertheless, Alva Ixtlilxochitl's decision to focus on Tetzcoco, and not Teotihuacan, as the subject of his histories is understandable. The town of

31. AGN-V (232:1, fol. 21r).

Teotihuacan was a small backwater and lacked the illustrious past for which Tetzcoco was famous. The well-known rulers of Tetzcoco were much better suited to the epic tone he chose for his narratives. Moreover, emphasizing his connection to such a distinguished lineage undoubtedly served to advance his professional career in a context where lineage and status were important.

Alva Ixtlilxochitl made a living employed in the burgeoning colonial bureaucracy of New Spain. He worked for a time as indigenous governor of several towns around Mexico City and later as an interpreter in the General Indian Court in the capital.[32] He was also an assiduous collector of native pictorial and alphabetic texts and a prodigious chronicler of Tetzcoca history, which he attempted to reconcile with the dominant political, religious, and intellectual currents from Western Europe. Alva Ixtlilxochitl is remembered today for his historical writings, and although his texts were not published in his lifetime, they were copied and quoted extensively over the years and have been among the most important sources for Mexican indigenous history for centuries.

The account of the conquest presented in the "Thirteenth Relation" of the *Compendio histórico del reino de Texcoco* (Historical compendium of the kingdom of Tetzcoco) is Alva Ixtlilxochitl's most widely printed and circulated text.[33] It was the first of his works to be published and the only one to have been translated. In 1829 Carlos María de Bustamante printed the text under the title *Horribles crueldades de los conquistadores de México*, which was translated and republished in France two years later as *Cruautés horribles des*

32. For a detailed chronology of the historian's life and times, see Alva Ixtlilxochitl (1975–77, 1:17–36). The jurisdictions of which Alva Ixtlilxochitl was governor included the city of Tetzcoco. Alva Ixtlilxochitl met with strong resistance from Tetzcoco's native nobles, however, and was removed from the post after little more than a month in office (AGN-IV 3066:8, fol. 1–2v). He was then appointed governor of the town of Tlalmanalco in the province of Chalco (AGN-I 9:17, fol. 9). For his work in the General Indian Court, see AGN-V (232, fol. 632–43).

33. Alva Ixtlilxochitl (1975–77, 1:415–521). Alva Ixtlilxochitl's magnum opus, *Historia de la nación chichimeca*, which covers the history of Tetzcoco from pre-Columbian times, includes a partial telling of the conquest up to the early stages of the siege of Mexico-Tenochtitlan (1975–77, 2:5–263). Alva Ixtlilxochitl's perspective on the conquest is notably different in the *Historia*, where Cortés is the main protagonist. For a comparative study of the two versions, see Brian (2010). For a study of the ways in which the two texts "claimed a historical share in the dominant values of Christian militancy," see Adorno (2007, 137–46).

conquérants du Mexique. In 1969 Douglass Ballentine published an English translation, which he titled *Ally of Cortés: Account 13, of the Coming of the Spaniards and the Beginning of the Evangelical Law.* Ballentine's text is out of print and difficult to find. More important, Ballentine had access only to a faulty nineteenth-century edition of Alva Ixtlilxochitl's works, which was based on copies of copies.

The translation presented in this volume is based on the holograph—the original, signed manuscript—of the "Thirteenth Relation." The original manuscripts of Fernando de Alva Ixtlilxo-chitl's five historical works had been lost to scholars until Wayne Ruwet located them in 1982, bound, along with various other texts, in a three-volume set that was part of the British and Foreign Bible Society collection.[34] The volumes had belonged to Mexican scholar Carlos de Sigüenza y Góngora (1645–1700), who was a friend of Alva Ixtlilxochitl's eldest son, don Juan de Alva. In the opening folio of the *Compendio histórico*, Sigüenza y Góngora noted that the text should be read with caution because on many occasions the author had disregarded the truth for the sake of aggrandizing his ancestor Fer-nando Cortés Ixtlilxochitl, who appears as the story's main character (fol. 1r). As with all the many and diverse versions of the conquest of Mexico produced during the sixteenth and seventeenth centuries, Alva Ixtlilxochitl's account betrays the biases of his own vantage point. Just as Hernando Cortés, Bernal Díaz del Castillo, the Tlate-lolca authors of the Florentine Codex, and Diego Muñoz Camargo were engaged in history writing motivated by a pragmatic context, don Fernando de Alva Ixtlilxochitl's history was also a product of his circumstances and part of an agenda to promote his own career within the colonial bureaucracy.

Nonetheless, the "Thirteenth Relation" transcends petty profes-sional ambitions and the "micropatriotic" rivalries of sixteenth-century central Mexico to add to our ever-expanding understanding of the history of the conquest and of the native communities and

---

34. The three volumes, which include manuscripts by Chimalpahin, Muñoz Camargo, and Alva Ixtlilxochitl as well as miscellaneous texts, were gifted to a repre-sentative of the Bible Society stationed in Mexico in the early nineteenth century. See Schroeder (1994) and Brian (2014b). Anderson and Schroeder published a transcription and translation of the third volume of manuscripts in a two-volume edition, *Codex Chimalpahin* (Chimalpahin 1997). In May 2014 the three volumes were sold by the Bible Society to Mexico's Instituto de Antropología e Historia (INAH).

Valley of Mexico
(ca. 1519)

Tollan

Atotonilco

Tolcayuca

Tlaquilpa

Tecpilpa

Tequizquiac

Hueypontla

Tezontepec

Tepexi

ACOLHUA

Huehuetoca

Tizayuca

Zumpango

Tecalco

Citlaltepec

Huitzila

Nopaltepec

Axapusco

Otumpan

Xaltocan

Cuauhtlatzingo

Tepozotlan

Teotihuacan

Cuauhtitlan

Oztoticpac

Toltitlan

Acolman

Cahuacan

Ecatepec

Tepexpan

Tecpan

Mazatla

Tepetlaoztoc

Tenayuca

Chiauhtla

TEPANECA

Tepeyacac

Tetzcoco

MEXICA

Huexotla

Azcapotzalco

Tlatelolco

Coatlichan

Tlacopan

Mexico-Tenochtitlan

Chimalhuacan Atenco

Coatepec

Atlacohuayan

Iztapalapa

Tetetlan

Coyoacan

Culhuacan

Iztapaluca

Tlaxcallan

Tlalpan

Atlapulco

Cuitlahuac

Xochimilco

Chalco

Mizquic

Tlalmanalco

Tenango

Amecameca

Xochitepec

Otzompa

Nepopohualco

Chimalhuacan

Totolapa

GULF OF
MEXICO

SOUTH
SEA

N

20 miles

The Mexico Basin is known locally as the Valle, or valley, de Mexico. Map by
Pablo García.

writers of the early colonial period. This edition of Alva Ixtlilxochitl's epic account of his ancestor Ixtlilxochitl furthers an important goal of conquest studies: to bring as many sides as possible to the conversation. Alva Ixtlilxochitl's Tetzcoca perspective—representing the second most important altepetl in the region at the time of contact—is an essential one. Admittedly, Alva Ixtlilxochitl makes the task of figuring out what happened during the conquest messy and somewhat more difficult. But it is precisely this difficulty that continues to attract us to the conquest as an object of study. Moreover, the dynamic plotline, full of passion and melodrama, propelled by the feats of the quintessential epic hero, has made this account a compelling story for centuries.

Thirteenth Relation: On the Arrival of the Spaniards and the Beginning of the Law of the Gospel

There was news of the coming of the Christians from some traders who had gone to the markets on the coast of Xicalanco, Ulua, and Champoton, especially when they bartered with Grijalva.[1] Thus, they held as very true the prophecies of their ancestors who predicted that this land would be possessed by the children of the sun.[2] Moreover, the omens that they observed in the sky pained them all greatly.[3] They took them to mean that their trials and persecutions were near; they called to mind the cruel wars and plagues suffered by their ancestors the Tolteca at the time of their destruction, which made them think that the same would happen to them. All this, however, did not trouble Moteczuma,[4] who found himself on the greatest throne that he or his ancestors had ever held. The whole empire

1. Juan de Grijalva led an expedition to the coast of the Yucatan peninsula in 1518. See Hassig (2006, 52–55.)

2. This is a reference to the Spaniards. In his "Third Letter" Cortés (1986, 258) claimed to have been addressed "as the child of the sun" during the siege of Mexico.

3. Book 12 of the Florentine Codex lists eight omens that signaled Mexico's impending doom. They include comets, temples being struck by lightning, mysterious weeping heard after dark, and the appearance of strange animals and monstrous beings. Lockhart (1993, 17) notes that no other Nahuatl source describes such phenomena. Alva Ixtlilxochitl's reference to omens suggests that he had access to a copy of Book 12, perhaps through his working relationship with the Franciscan friar Juan de Torquemada (ca. 1562–1624). On the two historians' collaboration, see León-Portilla (1979).

4. We have respected Alva Ixtlilxochitl's spellings of proper names. Where there is inconsistency, we have opted to use the most frequent spelling. For instance, Alva Ixtlilxochitl writes the name of the last Mexica emperor as both "Quauhtemoc" and "Cuauhtemoc." We have used a "Q" in the translation for consistency.

was in his hands: he lorded over all of Tezcuco[5] and its kingdoms and provinces because King Cacama[6] was his nephew and had been placed on the throne by his own hand, and the king of Tacuba[7] was Moteczuma's father-in-law and a very old man, who no longer had the strength to govern. And so, considering the great power he had, he did not believe that he could be conquered by any ruler, even the greatest in the world.

In the year *ce acatl*, 1 Reed, our 1519[8]—which was, according to Nezahualcoyotl, when the Chichimeca Empire would be destroyed[9]— Teopilli, Moteczuma's governor in Cotozta, sent messengers ahead. After a day and a night they brought Moteczuma a painting and news about the coming of the Spaniards, and they said that the Spaniards wanted to see him, for they came as ambassadors of our lord Emperor Don Carlos.[10] Depicted in the painting were the shape and dress of the men, as well as their number, weapons and horses and ships, and everything else that they had brought. Having seen and heard Teopilli's message, Moteczuma sent a gift to Cortés and many apologies and offerings. Knowing that the children of the sun wanted to come to Mexico to see him did not sit well with him, and he sent word that the road was arduous and that there were a thousand other difficulties. This was not enough. Rather, it spurred on the Spaniards to seek out Moteczuma, especially when they found out from the lord of Zempoalan about the discord in this land. The lord

5. Tetzcoco. The spelling of Tetzcoco varied widely in the early colonial period. "Tetzcoco" was the most common spelling employed by native writers, but "Tezcoco" and "Tezcuco" (used here by Alva Ixtlilxochitl) were also frequently employed. The name of the contemporary city is spelled "Texcoco" in Mexico today.

6. For the sake of simplicity, we have removed the reverential ending -*tzin* from the most commonly known Nahua names.

7. The Spanish distortion of Tlacopan.

8. Mesoamerican cultures developed a highly sophisticated calendric system. On the Nahua calendar, see Hassig (2001).

9. All of Alva Ixtlilxochitl's historical works are dedicated to recounting the saga of the legendary southern Chichimeca Empire founded by Xolotl, the first Gran Chichimeca. Xolotl's heirs became the dynastic rulers of Tetzcoco. The most important of these was Nezahualcoyotl (r. 1431–72), who, according to Alva Ixtlilxochitl, possessed the gift of prophecy and foresaw the Spanish conquest. While Nezahualcoyotl continues to be regarded as an exemplary figure, Lee (2008) argues that the tlatoani's standard characterization, which is largely based on Alva Ixtlilxochitl's s portrayal, is fraught with anachronisms, misinterpretations, and cultural inconsistencies.

10. King Charles I of Spain (r. 1516–56), who was also Charles V of the Holy Roman Empire (r. 1519–56).

of Zempoalan also offered to support Cortés and provide reinforcements. From here they went to Quiyahuiztan and other places until they reached Tlaxcala.[11] Everywhere they went, the locals greeted them with much joy and celebration, without any hostility. What hostility there was, was provoked by the Spaniards. Finally, after many other events, our men traveled all the way to Ayutzinco, where King Cacama came out to greet them and offer them his city of Tezcuco should they want to go there. The Spaniards, especially Captain Cortés, thanked him profusely for the offer and told him that it was not necessary because they were on their way to see Moteczuma, but that at another time he would accept the invitation.

Cacama returned to Tezcuco and from here he went to Mexico by boat.[12] Upon arriving, he informed Moteczuma about all that he had seen and how the Spaniards were already very close, because by this time they were already in Iztapalapan. Many times Moteczuma sought council as to whether it would be good to receive the Christians.[13] His brother Cuitlahua and other lords were of the opinion that it was not a good idea. Cacama was of the opposite opinion, saying that it was unbecoming for a ruler not to receive the ambassadors of another, especially in this case, because, according to the Christians, theirs was the greatest ruler in the world, as indeed our lord Emperor Don Carlos was. However, the outcome was predetermined,[14] and so the next day Moteczuma came out with his nephew Cacama and his brother Cuitlahua and all his court to receive Cortés, who at the time was where the chapel of San Antón[15] now sits. After welcoming him, Moteczuma took Cortés to his house and lodged him in the houses of his father, King Axayaca.[16] He gave Cortés many gifts and offered to be the emperor's friend and accepted the law of the

---

11. Located about seventy miles to the east of Mexico-Tenochtitlan, Tlaxcala was independent of the Triple Alliance at the time the Spaniards arrived.

12. Throughout the text "Mexico" refers to Mexico-Tenochtitlan, which later became Mexico City. It is never used here to mean the modern country of Mexico. Mexico-Tenochtitlan was on an island; Tetzcoco was located across the lake to the east (see map 1).

13. That is, the Spaniards.

14. As a logical corollary to the omens noted earlier, the notion of a predetermined outcome can be understood as an attempt to explain the conquest after the fact (Lockhart 1993, 17).

15. The chapel of San Antonio Abad in the Xoloco district of the city.

16. Axayacatl (r. 1469–81), sixth tlatoani of Mexico-Tenochtitlan.

Gospel.[17] Moteczuma provided many people from Tezcuco, Mexico, and Tlacopan to attend to the Spaniards.

After the Spaniards had spent four comfortable days hosted and entertained by the Mexica,[18] Cortés seized Moteczuma under some unknown pretext, proving what they say about all cruel men being cowards. Though in truth, it was the will of God that had come to pass, otherwise it would have been impossible for four Spaniards to hope to dominate such a large new world with so many thousands of people as there were at that time. Amazed by such arrogance, the nobles and the Mexica[19] captains withdrew to their houses. King Cacama ordered his brother Prince Nezahualquentzin and other nobles to take very good care of the Christians, give them everything they needed for their sustenance, and give them gold and other things if they should ask for them. The rest of the Mexica and Tepaneca,[20] seeing how their king had been imprisoned, no longer wanted to come serve the Spaniards.

The Spaniards had spent forty-six days in Mexico when Cortés asked Cacama to allow him to send certain Spaniards to his city of Tezcuco. Cortés requested that some nobles in Cacama's service accompany them to tour the city so that the people would not mistreat them. Cacama was pleased to do so. He commanded two of his brothers to go with them; one was Nezahualquentzin and the other was Tetlahuehuezquititzin. They were to entertain them and not anger them in any way and give them a large chest or trunk—which was two arms' lengths long, one arm's length wide, and as tall as a man—filled with gold items and jewels for them and their captain. As they were on their way to the canal next to Nezahualcoyotl's palaces to board the canoes, a servant of Moteczuma reached them with word that they should try to send those Spaniards away quickly

17.   The law of the Gospel refers to the whole of Christian life and practice, including all the obligations of being a Christian and the precepts of the Church, such as Mass attendance, regular confession, and prayer (Stafford Poole, e-mail correspondence, July 18, 2013).

18.   We have chosen to use "Mexica" where Alva Ixtlilxochitl uses "mexicanos" to avoid any confusion with modern Mexicans. The term initially designated the people living on the island shared by Tenochtitlan and Tlatelolco (Lockhart 1993, 22).

19.   In Nahuatl, ethnonyms usually end in -ca; people from Mexico are called Mexica, while people from Cholula are the Cholulteca.

20.   The Tepaneca occupied the western part of the Valley of Mexico, including the altepetl of Tlacopan and Azcapotzalco.

and give them all the gold they wanted, because perhaps with this the Spaniards' captain might release Moteczuma and the Spaniards might go back to their land. When he saw Nezahualquentzin talking with Moteczuma's servant, one of the Spaniards assumed that they were plotting to kill them. He beat this prince, who had done nothing worthy of punishment or given offense, and took him as a prisoner to Cortés, who had him publicly hanged.[21] King Cacama was greatly angered, and, had it not been for Moteczuma, who tearfully pleaded with him not to do anything, it would have been disastrous.

Cacama bore it as best he could and sent another one of his brothers named Tecpacxuchitzin with these Spaniards, who numbered twenty, to provide the ransom that they had asked of him. And so they gave them the filled trunk and returned to Mexico. Cortés said that it was not enough and that they should bring more. Therefore, Cacama sent for more, and they brought another full chest. Seeing the treasure that had been brought and having been informed about the great power and eminence of the king of Tezcuco, Cortés had King Cacama seized through trickery, making it appear that the order had come from his uncle Moteczuma. Cortés imprisoned Cacama securely with many guards. He told him that he would release him if he brought some lords of his lineage, some of his brothers, as hostages, which he did. Cacama gave Cortés four princes who were his brothers as well as some noble kinsmen as hostages. The Mexica and the Tlacopaneca were also forced to give hostages; the Spaniards believed that this would secure their position.

A few days into the Spaniards' stay in Mexico, Cortés received news that certain ships had arrived at the port.[22] He told the two kings, Moteczuma and Cacama, that it was in his best interest to go

---

21. In the *Historia de la nación chichimeca,* Alva Ixtlilxochitl (1975–77, 2:222) refers to some "relaciones de la ciudad de Tetzcuco" (accounts from the city of Tetzcoco) as the source for this anecdote, which is not related by Cortés, Gómara, or Díaz del Castillo. Placed later in the sequence of events, the hanging of Nezahualquentzin is mentioned without further explanation in the anonymous Tlatelolco account of 1528 (León-Portilla 1962, 129). On the other hand, Antonio de Herrera y Tordesillas (1726–30, 1:217) relates that Cacama hanged an unidentified servant for hiding from the Spaniards that he was supposed to guide to Tetzcoco. Alva Ixtlilxochitl names Herrera y Tordesillas as one of his sources (1975–77, 2:235).

22. The Port of Veracruz. This is the expedition led by Pánfilo de Narváez, who was charged with arresting Cortés and returning him to Cuba. Cortés, however, managed to arrest Narváez and persuade Narváez's men to join him.

meet the ships personally. Cortés asked them to give him a number of warriors, and he explained why he needed them. The kings answered that if it was for the purpose of fighting Christians, they absolutely could not provide them, but if it were to fight a different nation then in that case they would give him whatever he needed. If the Christians, those who had come, waged war against Cortés, they would support him fully and advise their governors to help him if he needed it, but otherwise they could provide him only with servants and porters for the road. As a result of this, Cortés took the laborers and servants given to him, ordered some of the treasure he had received to be taken, and left for the port, leaving Captain Alvarado in charge in his absence. Before he left, Moteczuma told Cortés that the Mexica were about to celebrate the very solemn feast of Toxcatl[23] and that he should allow it. Cortés replied that they could do as they wished since they were in their homeland and to rejoice, for it would please him greatly. Moteczuma told Cortés about this so that he would tell the remaining Spaniards not to be alarmed, since previously Cortés had toppled their idols and had told them not to hold sacrifices anymore: they wanted to hold the ceremony to please and placate their vassals, because they were all offended that their kings were treated like prisoners by four foreigners.

Cortés left, and the festival, which falls on May 19, at the beginning of their fourth month, called Toxcatl, came around. The night before, they lit paper lanterns and played their instruments as was their custom, and on the day of the festival they did the dance they call *macehualiztli*. More than a thousand noblemen came out to the courtyard of the main temple, each wearing the best jewels and ornaments they owned, without weapons or any protection whatsoever. The Tlaxcalteca, who were in the city, remembering similar celebrations during which they were sacrificed by the thousands, went to Captain Alvarado and gave false testimony about the Mexica, saying that they were preparing to come together to kill the Spaniards.[24] Alvarado believed it. He went to the temple to confirm that this was so and to see if they

23. A festival in honor of the god Tezcatlipoca, Toxcatl was held during the solar calendar month of the same name.

24. The Tlaxcalteca were often portrayed negatively in indigenous accounts of the conquest not because they were regarded as traitors but because there was a perception that they were rewarded more generously than other native groups for assisting the Spaniards against the Mexica (Lockhart 1991, 25).

were armed. Although he saw that they were all unarmed and not prepared for combat, he coveted the gold that they wore and placed ten armed Spaniards at each door. Then he entered the courtyard and temple with some other Spaniards, killed almost everyone who was inside, and took what they had on them. Upon seeing their lords killed without cause, the Mexica assembled their forces and chased the Spaniards into the palace, in which they barricaded themselves. At this point the Mexica would surely have killed all the Spaniards, without letting anyone escape, had Moteczuma not calmed their anger.

Cortés returned to Mexico and passed through the city of Tez-cuco, where he was received by some nobles, because Nezahualpilli's sons—the legitimate ones[25]—had been hidden by their vassals, and the others were being held hostage in Mexico. Cortés entered Mexico on the feast day of Saint John the Baptist[26] with all the army of Spaniards and allies from Tlaxcala and other places, without anyone barring his way.

Even though they provided all that the Spaniards required, the Mexica and the rest saw that the Spaniards did not want to leave their city or release their kings. So they gathered their soldiers and started making war on the Spaniards the day after Cortés entered Mexico; it lasted for seven days. On the third day, seeing his vassals' determination, Moteczuma stood on a high place and reprimanded them. The Mexica insulted him, calling him a coward and an enemy of his homeland, and even threatened him with their weapons. Here, they say, one of them hit him with a stone from which he died, although his vassals say that the Spaniards themselves killed him and stabbed him in his lower parts with a sword.[27] After seven days and

25. The distinction is anachronistic. Nahua family systems did not distinguish between legitimate and illegitimate offspring (Aguilar-Moreno 2006, 352). Alva Ixtlilxochitl calls the children born to Nezahualpilli's high-ranking wives "legitimate," while those born to mothers of less prestigious backgrounds he dubs "illegitimate."

26. June 24.

27. Spanish accounts agree that Moteucçoma's death resulted from being struck by a rock (Cortés 1986, 132; Gómara 1979, 202). Díaz del Castillo (2009, 223) and Herrera y Tordesillas (1726–30, 1:267) claim that the wound was not fatal but that Moteucçoma was so deeply saddened that he let himself die by refusing treatment and nourishment. On the other hand, reports of indigenous origin consistently accuse the Spaniards (Acosta 2002, 440; Chimalpahin 1997, 2:37; Durán 1994, 545). Assessing the likelihood that Moteucçoma was strangled or stabbed by his captors, Hassig (2006, 113) argues that by this point the disgraced ruler was more of a liability than an asset to the Spaniards.

many great deeds, the Spaniards abandoned the city along with their friends the Tlaxcalteca, Huexotzinca, and other nations, fleeing on the causeway that goes to Tlacopan. According to don Alonso Axayaca and some reports by native witnesses, before leaving the city, the Spaniards killed King Cacama and three of his sisters and two of his brothers, who had managed to survive until then. Many Spaniards and allies died as they retreated, until they reached a hill near Tlacopan; from here they turned to go toward Tlaxcala.

Once the Spaniards had left for Tlaxcala and twenty days had passed since Moteczuma's death, the Mexica crowned his brother Cuitlahua as their king. Cuitlahua asked the grandees of the kingdom of Tezcuco to determine who should rightfully inherit the throne of that kingdom and to crown him. They answered that it was not yet time because Yoyontzin, Nezahualpilli's youngest legitimate son, was too young.[28] Cuitlahua commanded, therefore, that Cohuanacoch, one of the legitimate sons, should govern, and they began gathering warriors in case the Spaniards came back. King Cuitlahua did not govern longer than forty days because he soon died from smallpox, which was spread by a black man.[29] Afterward, the Mexica swore their allegiance to King Quauhtemoc, the son of King Ahuitzotl[30] and the heiress of Tlatelulco. After many days spent in Tlaxcala territory recovering from his past struggles, Cortés fought some battles against the people of Tepeaca, Itztzocan, Quauhquechulan, and other places subject to the cities of Mexico and Tezcuco with the help of the lords of Tlaxcala, Huexotzinco, and Cholula. Cortés easily conquered them and secured their loyalty.[31] Seeing that he had a very large

---

28. Here, Alva Ixtlilxochitl suggests that Nezahualpilli named the youngest of his children, Yoyontzin, as heir. However, in the *Historia de la nación chichimeca* (1975–77, 2:189) he does not.

29. The introduction of smallpox was commonly attributed to a black slave brought by Pánfilo de Narváez (Durán 1994, 563; Gómara 1979, 194). At the time Narváez was sent to arrest Cortés, the disease was ravaging Cuba and Hispaniola (Cook 1998, 64).

30. Eighth tlatoani of Mexico-Tenochtitlan (r. 1486–1502).

31. The *Lienzo de Quauhquechollan,* a pictographic narrative produced in the early 1530s, depicts the establishment of the Spanish-Quauhquecholteca alliance as a peaceable agreement between equals (Asselbergs 2008, 142). Asselbergs (2008, 43–44) asserts that the Mexica kept defensive garrisons in Tepeaca, Itzocan, and Quauhquechollan at a high cost to the local populations, fueling resentment and driving the Quauhquecholteca to seek an alliance with Cortés. See Cortés 1986, 148.

number of allies and that almost everyone in the land was on his side, he decided to attack Mexico.

Cortés left Tlaxcala on the Day of the Innocents,[32] with 40 horsemen, 540 footmen and 2,500 Tlaxcalteca, Huexotzinca, Cholulteca, Tepeaca, Quauhquechulteca, Yztzoca, Chalca, and those from other parts that he chose.[33] He did not want to bring more, because Tecocoltzin, son of Nezahualpilli, who was one of the hostages King Cacama had given to him, told Cortés that in Tezcuco he would find all the people that he might need. Moreover, through certain messengers from Tezcuco, especially one named Quiquizca, the Princes Ixtlilxochitl, Tetlahuehuezquititzin, Yoyontzin, and the rest of the brothers offered their allegiance to Cortés despite the fact that their brother Cohuanacoch was lord of Tezcuco and a Mexica ally. When Quiquizca returned to Tezcuco to report on his mission, Cohuanacoch had him killed.

Once Cortés reached Cohuatepec, three leagues[34] outside Tezcuco, four high-ranking nobles came out to greet him on behalf of Cohuanacoch. As a token of good will, they gave him a small flag on a gold staff encrusted with many jewels. They told him how their lord had sent them to welcome him and invite him to take his entire army to stay in Tezcuco, where he would be comfortably housed and attended to. According to don Alonso and Chichinchicuatzin, a high-ranking captain who was one of the ambassadors present and to whom Cortés showed some respect, Cortés answered angrily that he did not want to have them as allies unless they first returned what they had taken from the forty-five Spaniards and three hundred Tlaxcalteca whom they had killed. The emissaries answered that neither their lord Cohuanacoch nor the city were to blame for this. Those responsible were certain servants of King Cacama who had done it to avenge their lord, who was prisoner at the time. The emissaries said they would deliver Cacama's servants in chains to satisfy Cortés. Then

32. December 28.
33. Restall and Asselbergs (2007, 17) explain that a Mesoamerican city-state faced two choices when threatened by another: fight to the end at the risk of an injurious defeat or come to relatively favorable terms with the aggressor. After testing their latest adversaries' combined strength, many smaller polities quickly chose the second option, perhaps thinking that joining the new coalition would help them break away from Mexica authority and eventually benefit from joint conquest ventures.
34. A league is a measure of distance equivalent to about three miles.

Cortés answered that he also knew that Cohuanacoch was on King Quauhtemoc's side and had ordered his brother Quiquizca killed for having gone to Tlaxcala to offer his brothers' allegiance on their behalf. Having heard these and many other explanations, the emissaries returned to Tezcuco and gave a full report to their lord. Seeing Cortés's determination, Cohuanacoch left with as many people as he could and went to Mexico to support King Quauhtemoc.

When Cortés was nearing Tezcuco, some nobles came out to greet him, including Prince Ixtlilxochitl and the rest of his brothers who were there. Cortés was pleased to see them. They told him about all that was happening and how their brother Cohuanacoch had gone to Mexico. Once in the city, they housed the Spaniards in King Nezahualcoyotl's palaces, where there was ample room for the whole army. Every day they spent in this city they were given everything they needed. On the very day that Cortés arrived in Tezcuco, he was informed how the residents were leaving and going to Mexico in canoes. Cortés ordered some nobles to call to them and make them come back and to tell them not to worry about Cohuanacoch because the rest of their lords, the princes of Tezcuco, were with Cortés, and Cortés would crown as their king and natural lord[35] the one who had the most right to the title, or whomever they pleased. This was agreeable to everyone, and soon almost all the residents came back to their houses and city. Everyone agreed to make Tecocoltzin their lord, even though he was King Nezahualpilli's illegitimate son, because they did not dare nominate the legitimate ones until they saw how these things would turn out (figs. 2a–b).

Tecocoltzin began his rule with good judgment. He sent his messengers to all the kingdoms and provinces subject to the kingdom of Tezcuco, especially to those that he knew had not sided with the Mexica, and spent the following eight days fortifying the city in case the enemies should want to besiege them. At the end of this period, Cortés wanted to see if he could take Iztapalapan, a well-fortified place that would be strategically valuable. So he left with as many as fifteen horsemen, two hundred Spaniards, and six thousand Aculhua,[36]

35. According to medieval Castilian law, a natural lord is one who is entitled to rule by right of his superior station and superior qualities and whose dominion is widely recognized by his vassals as well as by other lords (Chamberlain 1939, 130).

36. People from Aculhuacan, the region around Tetzcoco (see map 1).

FIG. 2A Tlotzin Map, detail. The succession of Tetzcoca rulers from 1515 to 1539, including (*right to left*) Cacama, Cohuanacoch, Tecocoltzin, Ixtlilxochitl, Yoyontzin, and Tetlahuehuetzquititzin. Photo courtesy of and copyright by the Bibliothèque Nationale de France.

FIG. 2B Tlotzin Map, detail. Drawing by Pablo García.

Tlaxcalteca, and other allied nations. When they reached Iztapalapan, the Mexica, who already knew about the attack, came out to meet them. They had a fierce and hard-fought battle on that day. But, because the people of Iztapalapan had their houses on small islands on the water, the Spaniards could not take them or do them harm. They wanted to remain there that night, but the Mexica prevented it by breaking up the causeway that held back much water.[37] If the Spaniards had not left in a hurry they would have all drowned there. The Mexica followed them as they retreated, killing many of the allies because they were protecting the Christians. Only one Spaniard died, because he was more reckless than the others.

Here, Ixtlilxochitl, who was leading the Aculhua, greatly distinguished himself. He single-handedly killed many enemy captains. It pained Quauhtemoc to find out that one of the legitimate princes of Tezcuco had distinguished himself so much, considering that it was to the advantage of the Christians and damaging to the Mexica. Furthermore, Ixtlilxochitl had opposed them in Otumpan,[38] Atenco, Cohuatlichan, and other places that the Mexica wanted to punish for their support of the Christians, gallantly defending these places. And for the reasons mentioned earlier, King Quauhtemoc and Cohuanacoch sent their bravest captains, offering to reward greatly the one who could capture or kill Ixtlilxochitl. A very brave warrior, a descendant of the royal house of Iztapalapan, committed himself to the task and promised the kings to bring Ixtlilxochitl to Mexico as his prisoner.

Tecocoltzin ordered many quilts,[39] shields, arrows, clubs, throwing spears, and other types of weapons and ammunition to be made for his own people as well as for the Spaniards. He also commanded that maize, chickens,[40] and other necessities for the army's sustenance be gathered in great amounts. Likewise, he readied all his vassals so that they would be ready when called. While he ordered and did all these things, Ixtlilxochitl was told that the brave captain from Iztapalapan had promised to take him to Mexico as a prisoner. He was upset by

37. Mexico was connected to the lakeshore by a system of causeways that also functioned as dikes.

38. Otumba.

39. Nahua warriors used stiff quilted-cotton shirts as armor, which are called *ichcahuipilli* in Nahuatl (Aguilar-Moreno 2006, 115).

40. Probably turkeys. Chickens arrived in the Americas only with the Europeans.

this information and issued a challenge to him. The two of them met in battle on the fields of Iztapalapan, and neither army was to interfere. Ixtlilxochitl handily defeated his opponent and bound his hands and feet. Afterward, he had dry reeds brought, threw them on him, and burned him alive. Ixtlilxochitl told the Mexica to tell their lord Quauhtemoc and his own brother Cohuanacoch that before allowing himself to be caught, he would do to them as he had done to their captain.

While these things were happening, Tecocoltzin, who had been baptized and given the name don Fernando—and was the first of this name in Tezcuco—died, to the great sorrow of the Spaniards because he was extremely noble and loved them very much. Don Fernando Tecocoltzin was handsome, tall, and very white, as white as the whitest Spaniard; his person and stature reflected his exalted lineage. He spoke the Castilian language, and so, on most nights, after dinner, Tecocoltzin and Cortés discussed everything that should be done regarding the wars. Owing to his sound judgment and diligence, they readily agreed on all matters.

Then the Aculhua chose Ahuaxpitzactzin, who later was called don Carlos, as their lord. He was one of the illegitimate princely sons of King Nezahualpilli. Don Carlos governed just a few days because, at the request of Cortés and the rest, they quickly made Ixtlilxochitl lord. This was done because he was so brave and was one of the legitimate sons whom all the natives respected due to the quality of his person. As I have said, his vassals had not wanted him until then because he was legitimate.[41] He finished doing what his brother Tecocoltzin had begun. He made the canal for the brigantines with his vassals and helped finish these ships[42] with the wood brought from Tlaxcala by nearly twenty thousand warriors from Tlaxcala, Huexotzinco, and Cholula.

Four days later Cortés, Ixtlilxochitl, and the rest of the lords agreed that while the canal was being dug, they would pay a visit to Mexico and see if Quauhtemoc and Cohuanacoch and the rest would want to surrender. Ixtlilxochitl took sixty thousand of his vassals and

41. Alva Ixtlilxochitl implies here that Ixtlilxochitl's vassals were keeping his high status hidden until after they knew Cortés's intentions.
42. Cortés was building sailing ships (brigantines) for attacking Mexico-Tenochtitlan from the water.

Cortés three hundred Spaniards and the twenty thousand Tlaxcalteca to go to Xaltocan, a place subject to the city of Tezcuco. The town was in revolt and had sided with Cohuanacoch. Cortés and Ixtlilxochitl took control of Xaltocan and then passed through Tultitlan, Tenayuca, and Azcapotzalco with very little resistance until they reached Tlacopan. It was the third day after having left Tezcuco. The people of Tlacopan, who were already prepared, came out to meet them, and they had a cruel battle, but our people were so skilled that they defeated the Tepaneca and won the city of Tlacopan, killing as many as they could. Seeing that night was coming, they withdrew into the palaces of King Totoquihuaztli I[43] before night fell. At dawn, they sacked the city and burned as many of the best houses and temples as they could. For six days they remained here, and each day they went out to fight and skirmish against the Mexica, always attempting to meet King Quauhtemoc to negotiate his surrender. Realizing that they could not, they returned to Tezcuco the same way they had come. Two leagues beyond Tlacopan, in open country, the Mexica, thinking that they were fleeing from them, caught up with them and they fought another fierce battle. The Mexica were defeated and quickly retreated to Mexico. After this, they went on to Aculma, where they slept for the night. The next day they arrived in Tezcuco, where twenty thousand men from Tlaxcala and other places asked Cortés for permission to leave, and they returned to their lands rich with plunder, which was what they always sought.

The men from Chalco came to warn Ixtlilxochitl that the Mexica sought to destroy them because Chalco was very important for providing essential supplies to the city of Tezcuco and the Spaniards. The Chalca requested that he send some captains and people and supplies to help them since they were under his dominion. They also requested that Ixtlilxochitl ask Cortés to send some Spaniards as well. Ixtlilxochitl informed Cortés, who sent three hundred Spaniards and fifteen men on horseback under the command of Gonzalo de Sandoval, along with eight thousand Aculhua vassals of Ixtlilxochitl under the command of the great captain Chichincuatzin. When they got to Chalco, where the people were already prepared and on their side, men from Huexotzinco and Quauhquechulan joined the Spaniards and

---

43. Tlatoani of Tlacopan and one of the founders of the Triple Alliance, along with Nezahualcoyotl of Tetzcoco and Itzcoatl of Mexico.

Aculhua, and they went to Huaxtepec, where the Mexica army was. Before they reached this place, the Mexica came out to meet them and fought bravely against them, but our people quickly defeated them and entered this town, where they seized and killed a great number of Mexica and took control of the whole place. While they were distracted, the Mexica and the Huaxtepeca, who were especially eager, attempted to retake control of the town. They got all the way to the central square in their attempt to force out the Spaniards and Aculhua, who came to meet them. They fought until the Mexica were driven out, and they chased them more than a league, killing many of them.

The Spaniards and the Aculhua spent two days in Huaxtepec and from there moved on to Acapichtlan, a well-defended place where there was a large army. Here they fought the enemy after having asked them to surrender. Both the Spaniards and their native allies fought hard here, and they took this place. They killed a large number of the enemy, and others drowned in the river that runs through Acapichtlan. Having taken this place, they all returned to their lands. With the Spaniards and some of the Aculhua, Sandoval returned to Tezcuco, while the rest remained in Chalco. Seeing that he could not defeat the Chalca, Quauhtemoc set about organizing a large army to attack and destroy them before they could get reinforcements. The Chalca found out that the Mexica were coming when it was almost too late. So they joined with some of their neighbors and the Aculhua who had stayed behind and came out to meet them and fought until they had defeated them. They killed a great many of them and captured forty captains, and the Chalca caught the general.

All the cities, towns, and places around Xochimilco, Cuitlahuac, Mizquic, Coyoacan, Culhuacan, Iztapalapan, Mexicatzinco, and the others allied with Mexico gathered more than sixty thousand warriors and attacked again to see if they could finally defeat Chalco. Since the Chalca knew about this, they made all the necessary preparations. They sent word to Ixtlilxochitl and the Spaniards to assist them. It was necessary, therefore, for Cortés to go personally with three hundred companions and thirty men on horseback and Ixtlilxochitl with more than twenty thousand of his vassals and some Tlaxcalteca who happened to be at hand. They spent the night at Tlalmanalco, which bordered the Chalca army's encampment. The next day nearly fifty thousand more men arrived; Ixtlilxochitl had summoned them from Tezcuco's nearby subject provinces.

The following day, as soon as they heard Mass, they left to fight their enemies, who were on a rocky hill that was very high and craggy. The women and children were at the summit, the soldiers and warriors were on the slopes. The Spaniards attacked on three sides. The vanguard was at great risk because those on top threw down many rocks and toppled those who attempted to ascend. They climbed a path that led to the top, but they were not able to ascend all the way because it was too rough and rocky. Many of our men[44] and two Spaniards died; more than twenty Spaniards were wounded. As they were attempting to ascend, they realized that the hill where they were fighting had been surrounded at the base by enemy forces. They were forced to climb back down and fight against those below in another cruel battle. However, the Spaniards quickly defeated them, and they went to spend the night on another rocky hill nearby. They encountered resistance in some places around there, but the enemy quickly fled. They spent the night here. The next day they returned to the first rocky hill, where the main enemy force was located. In a few hours they were able to locate a route by which they could take the hill. They climbed to the summit, and the enemy surrendered and asked for mercy. They were pardoned without being harmed. And they themselves sent word to their allies to surrender to the Christians and Aculhua, and so they did.

Our forces were in this place for two days. They sent the wounded to Tezcuco and left for Huaxtepec, where there was a large enemy army. Night had already fallen when they came to a large country estate,[45] and they spent the night there. The people there were unprepared, and they fled at dawn. Our forces pursued them as far as Xilotepec, where they killed many of their enemy, who were also unprepared. After witnessing this, those from Yauhtepec surrendered to our people. From Xilotepec they advanced on Quauhnahuac,[46] a large and strong city that is subject to Ixtlilxochitl's dominion. Since they were on the side of his brother Cohuanacoch and the Mexica, and therefore rebelling against him, Ixtlilxochitl ordered

44. Alva Ixtlilxochitl adopts the perspective of Tetzcoco here. "Our men" refers to the Aculhua. However, Alva Ixtlilxochitl's use of the inclusive plural varies and at other points comprises the Spaniards.

45. Probably the well-known country home of the Mexica rulers. The gardens and sulfur springs of Oaxtepec still attract weekend visitors from Mexico City.

46. Cuernavaca.

them to surrender. They did not want peace but war. And they got it. Advancing by a rough and challenging place—since there was not a better route—our people quickly defeated them. Those who were able to flee sought shelter up in the mountains nearby. The Spaniards burned the best places and houses. The lord of the province and the rest of his vassals, acknowledging their defeat, came and begged for mercy from Ixtlilxochitl. They also asked that Ixtlilxochitl convince the Christians to pardon them, for then they would be in their debt and would join them against the Mexica. Ixtlilxochitl was pleased and pardoned them because they were repentant about what they had done. He presented them to Cortés to be welcomed as allies.

After all this had happened, they returned to Xochimilco, and on the second day they reached the outskirts of the city, which was big and well fortified and surrounded by water. The inhabitants and the Mexica who supported them tore down the bridges and opened the canals and prepared to defend their city. They believed that they would not be defeated since there were many of them and they were in a strong position. Our men began to fight them, and they were so skillful that they took the first barricade that went up to the main bridge, the strongest in the city. The Xochimilca got into their canoes and fought until nightfall, at which time they moved their women, elderly, and belongings to a safe place. The next day the Xochimilca wanted to destroy the bridge, but they were chased out of the city. On the field, they fought valiantly as the warriors they were. They put our men in danger and almost captured Cortés when his horse fell from exhaustion. The Spaniards and Aculhua came and quickly gathered around him and put the enemy to flight. But they did not follow them; rather, the Spaniards returned to the city to fix the bridges, patching them with mud and stone. When they arrived, they found two dead Spaniards, who had disobeyed orders and had gone out plundering by themselves. Knowing this, Quauhtemoc immediately sent more than fifteen thousand warriors by water and by land. Our forces fought against them vigorously and defeated them, and the Spaniards burned the city's temples and houses. These and many other things of which I will not speak occurred on the fourth day after they occupied the city.

They left the city and went toward Culhuacan, which lay two leagues toward Mexico. The Xochimilca attacked them on the road. Our forces fought against them and quickly defeated them. When our forces arrived in Culhuacan, they found it abandoned. They rested here for two days, after which they thoroughly scouted the place in preparation for their siege of Mexico. They burned temples and palaces; then they turned to Mexico. They fought at the first barricade and managed to seize it only with much effort. Many natives died. Many Spaniards were wounded. From here they returned to Tezcuco, after having planned very carefully how they would enter the city, and set the brigantines on the lake. Many other things happened on this journey, during which numerous Aculhua and other allies died since they were on the front lines.

When they reached the city of Tezcuco, they found the canal nearly completed.[47] It was over half a league long and twelve or thirteen feet wide and more than twelve feet deep. It was reinforced, and on each side it had a retaining wall. It took fifty days and 400,000 men from the kingdoms of Tezcuco, whom Ixtlilxochitl had pressed into service for this purpose; they worked in shifts of 8,000 or 10,000 each day. Ixtlilxochitl also found in Tezcuco many lords from various provinces under his dominion. They had come to show their loyalty to him and ally themselves with the Christians in the ongoing war against the Mexica. Up to this point these lords had been in rebellion and allied with the Mexica. Ixtlilxochitl was very pleased to see them and commanded them to gather everything they needed, both people and supplies. He did the same all over the kingdom of the Aculhua, who were his vassals, and the other subject territories, telling them all to convene in Tezcuco in ten days. Cortés sent the lords of Tlaxcala, Huexotzinco, and Cholula with similar orders.

On the second day of Pentecost,[48] when all the army had gathered in Tezcuco, Cortés mustered the Spaniards. Ixtlilxochitl did the same. The army was made up of 200,000 warriors, along with 50,000 laborers, who were to repair the bridges and do other necessary jobs. The first 50,000 warriors were from Chalco, Itztzocan, Quauhnahuac, Tepeyacac, and other subject territories to the south; another 50,000 men were from the city of Tezcuco and its environs, not counting 8,000 Tezcuca captains who lived there; another 50,000 from the

---

47. Cortés was digging a canal from Tetzcoco to the lake through which to launch his fleet of brigantines.
48. Church feast celebrating the descent of the Holy Spirit. It is held fifty days after Easter.

provinces of Otumpan,[49] Tolantzinco, Xicotepec, and other territories
that likewise belonged to Tezcuco and are Aculhua; lastly, another
50,000 Tziuhcohuaca, Tlatlauhquitepeca, and people from other
northern provinces subject to the kingdom of Tezcuco. This, as I have
said, totals 200,000 warriors. Ixtlilxochitl ordered that all the canoes
in Tezcuco be brought together. He managed to get together sixteen
thousand canoes, some of which went with the brigantines, and the
rest carried the supplies for the army. On this day they reviewed the
Tlaxcalteca, Huexotzinca, and Cholulteca, each lord with his vassals.
All in all there were 300,000 warriors.

Seeing the multitude supporting him, Cortés, in agreement with
Ixtlilxochitl and the rest of the lords, divided the army in the following way: Pedro de Alvarado would go to Tlacopan with 30 men on
horseback, 170 Spanish foot soldiers, and 50,000 men from Otumpan, Tolantzinco, and other territories whom Ixtlilxochitl ordered to
go with them; their generals were his brother Quauhtliztactzin and
the lord of Chiautla, who was called Chichiquatzin. They were also
accompanied by the entire Tlaxcalteca army. Cortés gave the next
captain, Cristóbal de Olid, 33 men on horseback, 180 foot soldiers,
and two cannons—just as the previous company had—as well as
another 50,000 men from Tziuhcohuac and the rest of the northern
territories; their general was Tetlahuehuezquititzin, brother of Ixtlilxochitl, and other lords accompanied him. This group was ordered
to go to Culhuacan. The next captain, Gonzalo de Sandoval, received
23 horses, 160 foot soldiers, and another two cannons. Those from
Chalco, Quauhnahuac, and the rest of the southern territories, who
numbered another 50,000, were to aid them. Their own lords and
some of Ixtlilxochitl's brothers acted as their generals. The Cholulteca
and Huexotzinca also went with them. They were ordered to go to
Iztapalapan and destroy it and set up their encampment wherever
was most convenient for them. Among all the parties, 50,000 laborers
were divided to repair bridges and tear down others, both of which
were necessary things for the good of our forces. Cortés took control
of the brigantines, and made himself commander of the fleet. He was
accompanied by Ixtlilxochitl, who took sixteen thousand canoes carrying 50,000 Tezcuca vassals and 8,000 valiant captains to defeat the
forces on the lake and those up on the rocks.

49. Otumba.

No one slept in Mexico. The kings Quauhtemoc, Cohuanacoch, and Tetlepanquetzal readied everything that was needed and fortified the city. They gathered almost 300,000 men to their side. They sent grave reprimands to Ixtlilxochitl for supporting the children of the sun and for turning against his own homeland and kinsmen. Each time, Ixtlil- xochitl replied that he would rather be a friend to the Christians, who brought the true light and whose mission was good for the salvation of the soul, than side with his homeland and kinsmen, who refused to obey them. Not only would Ixtlilxochitl support and aid the Chris- tians in all things, but he would give his life for them.[50] Everything he said infuriated the Mexica. Quauhtemoc and the other two, seeing the great forces that the Christians had with them and Ixtlilxochitl's resolve, returned to ask the Mexica people to surrender because the evidence clearly indicated that they would be vanquished. The Mexica insisted that they would rather die defending their homeland than be slaves to the children of the sun, who were cruel and greedy.

This and many other reasons forced Quauhtemoc and the others to continue with their plans, even though it was all in vain; the city of Tezcuco and all of its kingdoms and provinces, which were the most important and strongest, were on the side of the Christians. Tlaxcala, Huexotzinco, and Cholula were also on the side of the Christians, but this was of little consequence. As I have said, if Tezcuco had not joined them, the number of people that Tlaxcala, Huexotzinco, and Cholula provided would have been powerless against the three capi- tals of Tezcuco, Mexico, and Tlacopan. It is clear in the histories that the aid provided to the Spaniards by Ixtlilxochitl and his brothers and kinsmen, who were the lords and captains of the Tezcuca armies, was crucial and second only to God's. As I have stated, the law of the Gospel was established and the city of Mexico and other places were won with much less struggle and cost than would have been neces- sary without Tezcuco and its kingdoms and provinces.

At this point, while wars were being waged, Ixtlilxochitl ordered his brother Ahuaxpictzactzin to come urgently with food and

50. On the spiritual conquest of Mexico, see the classic work by Ricard (1966). For a reappraisal of the introduction and practice of Christianity among natives, see Burkhart (1989) and Tavárez (2011). Ixtlilxochitl's immediate and zealous embrace of Christianity is consistent with Alva Ixtlilxochitl's rewriting of the history of Tetzcoco as a preparation for the Gospel (*praeparatio evangelica*), owing mainly to Nezahualco- yotl's wisdom and foresight. See Velazco (2003).

weapons and everything necessary for both the Spaniards and his
army and to ready all the Aculhua and the rest of his subjects so that
they would be prepared in case help was needed. Ahuaxpictzactzin
did just as his brother commanded, so they lacked nothing for the
duration of the war for Mexico, as we will see. Cortés and the rest of
the Spaniards had spent five months in Tezcuco doing all the aforementioned things. Once they were all ready and fully equipped, they
left the city of Tezcuco with the whole army. They set out for Mexico
on the eleventh day of their third month, called *huey tozoztli*,
or Great Vigil, which is also the twelfth day of their week, the day
called *matlactli omome calli*, or 12 House, which, according to our
calendar, generally falls on the tenth of May.

The magnificent and powerful army, with each general and his
troops departing toward their assigned position, was one of the greatest sights this land had ever seen. Alvarado and Cristóbal de Olid
went by way of Aculma, where they camped for the night. Finding
little resistance along the way, they reached Tlacopan on the third
day after leaving Tezcuco. The next day Cristóbal de Olid and Tetlahuehuezquititzin and the other lords and captains left for Chapul-
tepec, where they broke the aqueduct, thereby depriving the Mexica
of water. The Mexica tried valiantly to defend it both by water and
by land but had little success because, though there were many of
them, they could not overcome the wrath of our men. Then our
forces went back to help Alvarado, who was clearing the way for the
horses, repairing bridges and other things, and filling in gaps. They
worked at this for three days and at great risk to the natives, many of
whom died fighting the enemy and from their labors. Likewise, many
Spaniards were wounded, but they took some bridges and barricades.
Once this was done, Alvarado stayed in Tlacopan with Iztocquauh-
tzin and the rest of the lords and captains. Olid went with the rest to
Culhuacan, capturing positions along the way. Here they garrisoned
themselves in the lordly houses and went out each day to fight the
Mexica. They did this for eight full days.

Gonzalo de Sandoval, along with those from Chalco and other
places, went to Iztapalapan and started fighting as soon as they got
there. The residents of Iztapalapan defended themselves for as long
as they could, and they were so worn down by our forces that they
left the city and went to Mexico with their women and children.
When Sandoval and the others saw that those from Iztapalapan had

abandoned the place, they entered and burned many houses and temples, so the enemy would have no shelter to return to. Cortés with his brigantines and Ixtlilxochitl with his army's sixteen thousand canoes advanced on Mexico. The first battle was on the big rocky hill, where there were a great many warriors and women and children. They climbed up to the summit with great effort because it was rough and high, and at the top was a large enemy force. They fought against them and won. They killed everyone; only the women and children were left alive. This came at great cost to our forces because many died and twenty-five Spaniards were wounded.

Having been warned by the people on the big rocky hill that the Christians were advancing on Mexico in brigantines and canoes, the Mexica went out to meet them. The Spaniards were still on the hill when five hundred Mexica canoes, the best there were, came forward to fight and assess the enemy. Once they were near our canoes they decided to wait because, being tired and few, they felt they were not ready for battle. After a while, so many canoes had gathered that they covered almost the entire lake. Once our forces were ready for battle, a favorable wind rose up, which was of great significance. Cortés and Ixtlilxochitl quickly signaled their men, ordering them to come all at once and push the enemy back to Mexico. Once the order had been given, they all launched themselves at the canoes. The Mexica fought awhile, but when they saw that the wind was against them, they fled so hurriedly that their canoes collided with one another and broke or sank. Our forces killed everyone they could catch, though they put up a fight, and those who were able to escape were forced back into the city. Many nobles and captains and even some lords were captured. So many died that the big lake[51] was tainted with blood and looked nothing like water. With this victory, our forces were masters of the lake.

Meanwhile, Alvarado and Olid with the rest of their forces entered the causeways. They fought and took a number of bridges and barricades, no matter how tenaciously the Mexica defended them. Cortés and Ixtlilxochitl found no enemies on the water—they were too frightened to remain on the lake—so they went with their forces to help and quickly advanced. They jumped on the Iztapalapan

51. Lake Tetzcoco, the largest of five interconnected lakes at the center of the Mexico Basin, more commonly known as the Valley of Mexico.

causeway and fought for control of two towers, or temples, surrounded by stone walls. They managed to take them, but at great
risk, because inside were many enemies. They fired three cannon
shots that caused much damage and dislodged the enemy warriors
who were preventing our forces from advancing along the causeway.
And this is when the powder ran out. Since it was late, they stopped
fighting and decided to camp there for the night. That night Ixtlilxochitl sent for half the Chalca army, which was in Culhuacan; Cortés
likewise sent for fifty Spaniards and powder. The next day they
fought their enemy, seized a bridge, and followed them until they
reached the first houses in the city. Many great things happened here,
and many natives died on both sides.

Next to our forces' camp, the laborers whom Ixtlilxochitl had
brought broke part of the causeway so that four brigantines and five
thousand canoes could pass through and take control of the freshwater lake.[52] Once on this side of the causeway, they defeated all the
canoes they found there within a few hours and killed many people.
The next day their clashes with the enemy were worse than the ones
before. At this point Sandoval came with some Spaniards. Cortés,
in agreement with Ixtlilxochitl, had ordered him to leave the rest of
his native allies with Cristóbal de Olid. When Sandoval arrived with
his men to help Cortés, his foot was pierced during the fight. Many
others were wounded, and some natives died because they were
on the front lines. However, they skillfully managed to kill a great
number of the enemy. Ixtlilxochitl, who killed many on this day, cut
off the legs of a very brave Mexica captain in a single swipe, using a
sword given to him by Cortés.

Once nearly all the towns surrounding Mexico had been defeated
and destroyed, they organized their soldiers, set up their camps
where they thought best, and gathered supplies and other necessities; they busied themselves at this for six days. They found many
points through which the brigantines could enter the city, all the
while engaging in many skirmishes with the Mexica. The brigantines
and the Tezcuca canoes went deep into the city. They toppled many
houses in the outlying districts and burned down others. They then

---

52. The portion of Lake Tetzcoco to the west of the Ixtapalapa causeway.
By breaking the causeway, the brigantines would be able to sail more freely around
Mexico-Tenochtitlan.

laid siege to the city on four sides: Cortés and his great ally Ixtlilxochitl on the causeway that runs between the two lakes, next to the temples they had won in previous days; Pedro de Alvarado with his allies in Tlacopan; Cristóbal de Olid on the Coyohuacan causeway; and Gonzalo de Sandoval on the north side, keeping watch so that the enemy would not escape or be able to get supplies, weapons, or reinforcements from that direction.

One day, when everything was ready, they decided that they should all attack the city and win as much as possible in the following way: Cortés and Ixtlilxochitl by the causeway that now leads to San Antón; Pedro de Alvarado and Gonzalo de Sandoval, the west and the south, respectively. Cristóbal de Olid sent half of the Spaniards and some horses he had. He was ordered to guard the Culhuacan causeway with the rest of the Spaniards under his command and fifteen thousand allies so the Mexica would not receive aid from Xochimilco and other places. With the brigantines and canoes ready to protect the rearguard of our forces on both sides of the causeway, Cortés and Ixtlilxochitl left at dawn, one with more than two hundred Spaniards and the other with eighty thousand warriors. The enemy was well armed and waiting for them behind strong defenses, since they had broken a piece of the causeway and carved out the gap in such a way that no one would be able to cross it.

Ixtlilxochitl, who had with him twenty thousand men to repair the roads, ordered them to fill in the gap with stone and turf; they quickly patched it. This work was very difficult, because the enemy was pelting them with arrows and stones from the other side. Once the gap was repaired, they crossed over to fight with the enemy. After a few hours they defeated them and proceeded to the city's entrance. In a high tower next to a very high bridge, they barricaded themselves so that our forces would not take them. The brigantines and the canoes attacked this tower from the water, and with their help—which was very effective—they took it within a few hours. Then the entire army crossed to the other side on the brigantines and canoes, with most of the natives swimming across. Ixtlilxochitl ordered those in charge of repairing the roads to close this gap with stone and mud. With their men, he and Cortés advanced and won another barricade at the beginning of a broad, main street, on which they pursued the enemy to another gap, whose bridge was removed like the rest. The enemy crossed on a single beam, and, once across, they removed the beam; most of them crossed on the water.

Once our forces arrived, Ixtlilxochitl summoned half of those who were bridging the gap, since by now they were finishing their work. When they arrived, they began to bridge it with the help of many soldiers and at great risk. Many of the laborers died from the stones and arrows shot by countless enemy warriors from the other side and from the rooftops, even though many Spaniards were defending them with guns and crossbows. The Spaniards fired two cannon shots that did great harm to the enemy. Some of the soldiers crossed to the other side and fought against the Mexica, but the Mexica soon fled, since the gap had been bridged and the rest of the army crossed over. They pursued the enemy to another gap that was next to one of the city's main squares. Meeting little resistance, they entered a residential area. Though there were countless enemy warriors, they fought against them until they made them retreat in several directions; most of them fled to the main temple of Huitzilopoxtli. They chased them and entered the central courtyard, and after a short time they forced out as many as they could and killed the ones who resisted. They climbed the tower and toppled many idols, especially in Huitzilopoxtli's chapel. Cortés and Ixtlilxochitl arrived at the same time and rushed at the idol. Cortés grabbed the golden mask inlaid with precious stones that the idol was wearing; Ixtlilxochitl chopped off the head of the idol whom he had worshipped as his god just a few years before.

All this was accomplished at no small risk because their enemies kept throwing stones and arrows. Many Mexica captains valiantly defended the temple until they were driven out of the chapels. Quauhtemoc greatly reprimanded his forces for fleeing from the children of the sun and abandoning their idols. And so all the able enemy warriors joined together to fight against our forces until they made them flee. Cortés and Ixtlilxochitl held them back for a short while, and here Ixtlilxochitl killed the Mexica general who carried a Spanish spear that in previous days he had taken from a Spaniard whom he had killed. He struck him three times with the *macana*,[53] and with the last strike, he cut off half his head and an ear. When the enemy saw their dead general, they got so enraged that they

---

53. *Macuahuitl,* a club studded with obsidian blades.

charged our forces with such violence that they drove them back to the square. However, our forces managed to retake the temple, which they held until it got late, and they returned to their camp. On the way back Ixtlilxochitl ordered the houses on this street burned down. As our forces were leaving, so many enemy warriors rushed them that everyone would have been killed, but since the gaps had been bridged, they were able to retreat easily. Alvarado and Sandoval, with the rest of the allied lords, fought very well on this day, winning some bridges and barricades from the enemy.

The next day Ixtlilxochitl received fifty thousand reinforcements. They were all his Aculhua vassals, sent by his brother Ahuaxpi-tzactzin. Ixtlilxochitl took thirty thousand for himself and sent ten thousand to Alvarado and his forces; their leader was Quauhtliztac-tzin. He also sent Gonzalo de Sandoval another ten thousand because they were all in great need. Likewise, he ordered the five thousand warriors maimed and wounded in the previous battles to return to Tezcuco to recover. Some historians, especially Spaniards, write that Ixtlilxochitl came with his fifty-thousand-man army by order of his brother Tecocoltzin, which is completely wrong.[54] Tecocoltzin had died by this time, as I have already written, according to don Alonso Axayaca and native accounts and paintings, especially one that I own that is written in the Tolteca language, which they now call Mexican,[55] and signed by all the old nobles of Tezcuco and confirmed and certi-fied by all the other nobles and elders of this land. These sources are the ones I follow in my history because they are the truest, and the ones who wrote or painted them were personally present.[56] More-over, some of them have told me personally how it happened, because they died only a few years ago, and I met them when they were very old.

54. See Cortés (1986, 220), Gómara (1979, 258), and Herreray Tordesillas (1726–30, 2:32). Torquemada (1943, 1:548), on the other hand, confused Ixtlilxochitl and Cohuanacoch, alleging that the latter was sent as commander of the reinforce-ments and also took Fernando as his Christian name.

55. That is, Nahuatl.

56. Alva Ixtlilxochitl was an avid collector of historical documents. His archive included the Xolotl Codex, the Quinatzin Map, and the Tlotzin Map, which he used to compose the ancient history of Tetzcoco. The precise native sources for his account of the conquest have not been identified. Edmundo O'Gorman's edition of the *Obras históricas* includes a comprehensive registry of references; for the ones mentioned in the "Thirteenth Relation," see Alva Ixtlilxochitl (1975–77, 1:61–64).

Ixtlilxochitl came with Cortés and the rest of them when they left
Tezcuco, and he was physically present for all eighty days that the
war for Mexico lasted without missing a single one. He was on the
front lines during every battle, as a good captain should be. He risked
his life many times to save the Spaniards from their Mexica enemies.
If it had not been for Ixtlilxochitl and his brothers, kinsmen, and
vassals, the Mexica could have killed every single Spaniard on many
occasions, if it had not been for him, as I have told. It shocks me that
Cortés did not mention Ixtlilxochitl or his exploits or heroic deeds,
not even to the writers and historians, in spite of the fact that this
prince was the greatest and most loyal ally he had in this land and
whose aid in winning this land was second only to God's. Not only
did Ixtlilxochitl not receive any reward, but that which belonged to
him and his ancestors was taken away. And, even worse, they did not
leave even a few houses and a little land for his descendants to live
on. If I were to inform our lord the emperor about all these things,
I believe that not only would he reinstate that which was his, but he
would also grant him many and very distinguished favors. No one
recalls the Aculhua-Tezcuca and their lords and captains, even though
it is a single lordly house. Rather, they recall the Tlaxcalteca who,
as all the historians say, were more eager to plunder than to aid,
which is clear, since they even stole from the houses in the city of
Tezcuco and other places that were allied with the Christians. In particular, they pillaged the palaces of Nezahualpilli, where they burned
down the best rooms and part of the royal archives. The Tlaxcalteca
were the first to destroy the histories of this land. They are remembered, as everyone agrees, because wherever they went, they sought
to steal and loot whatever they found. And they gave all the gold
they took to the Spaniards. In sum, they plundered as much as they
could and sided with the Christians.

The Aculhua and their subject provinces, however, did not do
this. They had pity on the women, children, and elderly who begged
them to let them keep their belongings and be content with taking
the lives of their husbands, fathers, or sons. Moreover, many of the
Aculhua had kinsmen in Mexico. There were even some who fought
against their fathers, sons, and brothers; Ixtlilxochitl, his brothers,
and the other lords, in particular, fought against their own brothers,
uncles, and kinsmen. There were many times when Ixtlilxochitl was
fighting one of his relatives and the Mexica lords would insult him

from the rooftops, calling him a traitor against his homeland and kinsmen and making other offensive accusations. In truth, they were right. But Ixtlilxochitl stayed silent and fought because he valued the friendship, help, and safety of the Christians more than anything else, which made King Quauhtemoc very sad, since it left little hope of defeating the Spaniards and liberating their homeland. The same could be said of Cohuanacoch, lord of Tezcuco—though in name only, since he had nothing but the title—and of Tetlepanquetzal of Tlacopan, because the full power of Tezcuco, its kingdoms, and provinces were on the side of the Christians. This we have seen in this history and will see again in what remains to be said.

Likewise, it is well known that Chalco, Quauhnahuac, Itztzocan, Tepeacac, Tolantzinco, and other kingdoms and provinces that allied with our forces—excluding Tlaxcala, Huexotzinco, and Cholula—were subjects of Tezcuco. The histories state that these kingdoms sought the opinion of Tezcuco, which was their capital, before they allied with the Christians. Tezcuco's subject kingdoms aided the Spaniards by order of Tecocoltzin and Ixtlilxochitl, whom they obeyed as the sons of their king Nezahualpilli. According to the histories, and as everyone knows, if these kingdoms had not been the subjects of the kingdom of Tezcuco, it would have been impossible to bring them over to our side, and, if any of them had joined us, they would certainly have fought among themselves, which would have been a great hindrance.

Two days after the fifty thousand men from Tezcuco arrived, those from Xochimilco and some Otomí nations came to join Cortés, offering reinforcements and other war necessities. They begged Ixtlilxochitl to be their advocate so that Cortés would pardon their past deeds. Ixtlilxochitl spoke to Cortés, telling him that he should forget the past, that they would ally with him, and that they were very important allies because they lived along the lake and had many boats. Cortés was very pleased. He told them to go home and to return to camp in three days with as many people as they could muster and all the canoes they had so that they could fight on the canals and lakes with the brigantines and all the rest of Tezcuco's and Ixtapalapan's canoes. The Xochimilca did so and arrived at Cortés's camp on the assigned day. Every night they patrolled the lake around the city with those from Tezcuco, looking for anyone sneaking supplies into the city. They would kill them and seize all the supplies they had.

It had been five days since our forces had fought the enemy, who during this time had reopened the gaps that our forces had bridged. The enemy had also built better barricades and bulwarks than before, and they were well prepared with all the men and supplies that they needed. They howled in anticipation as they awaited our attack. After hearing Mass on this day, Cortés and Ixtlilxochitl left the camp with all their army by land and by water to advance on Mexico. The other captains did the same from their positions. At the first gap they reached, the army crossed over on the brigantines and canoes, and they fell upon the enemy, winning the gap and the barricade. They chased them to another gap, where the Mexica barricaded themselves, though our forces won it from them with much effort. Our forces followed them from one gap to the next until they reached the square. Ixtlilxochitl ordered the twenty thousand sappers to repair these bridges and fill up the gaps in the causeways, which took them almost the entire day. Cortés and Ixtlilxochitl fought very well against the enemy, a great many of whom died, as did some of our forces who were ambushed. It took a few hours to force them to retreat into their houses and temples, where they barricaded themselves.

Among the many whom he killed that day, Ixtlilxochitl killed a very brave captain, who was also his relative, at the entrance to the main temple. Ixtlilxochitl took away a Spanish sword that the captain carried, which he had taken from a Spaniard he killed a few days before. Likewise, he fought the general of the Mexica, who was very courageous. The general was wounded, though not fatally, and ran away to the palaces of Ixtlilxochitl's brother King Cacama. He barricaded himself inside with many of his captains. Ixtlilxochitl sought to enter to seize and kill him, but he could not because he found great resistance at the entrance and killed some who were defending it. Seeing that he would not be able to enter, and under pressure from his men to go aid some Spaniards who found themselves in a grave predicament while skirmishing with the enemy, Ixtlilxochitl turned around and went to help the Christians. They set fire to houses and temples, including the palaces of Axayaca and the aviary, which upset the Mexica greatly. Then they returned to their camp. When the Mexica saw our forces withdraw, they pursued them and they killed many Tlaxcalteca, who were loaded down with so much plunder that they were at the rear.

The following day, after all this had happened, our forces heard Mass before dawn. Then they went to the city, but despite the early hour, they found that the Mexica, as they usually did, had taken down the bridges and broken up the causeway in many places. The Mexica had not slept at all that night; King Quauhtemoc himself had been with them. On this day our forces spent much effort and almost all the ammunition and were not able to win more than two gaps. When they withdrew, there were some casualties inflicted by the Mexica, who thought they were fleeing. Meanwhile, Alvarado and Quauhtliztactzin won two other gaps and burned down many houses and killed many enemy warriors. The people of Cuitlahuac, Mizquic, Culhuacan, Mexicaltzinco, and Huitzilopoxco came to join Cortés; they asked Ixtlilxochitl to order his men, especially those from Chalco, not to harass them anymore because almost every day they plundered their houses. Ixtlilxochitl sent word to the lords of Chalco to order their men to stop mistreating them, because they were his allies and on the side of the children of the sun. They were also ordered to build houses along the causeway for the army, especially for the Spaniards, because the rainy season was near. And he told them to bring food and gifts for Cortés and his men and to bring all the canoes they had to join together with the others.

Later Cortés ordered the brigantines and canoes from Tezcuco and all the other places, which were in the freshwater lake, to surround the city on all sides, burn as many houses as they could, and kill or capture as many people as possible. Cortés, with Ixtlilxochitl and his army, entered the city and sought to win the Tlacopan causeway to be able to communicate with Alvarado, which would have been very useful. He set to work, as did Alvarado and Sandoval, with each advancing as far as they could. On this day Cortés was able to win only three gaps; he filled them up and returned to his camp. The next day he returned to the Tlacopan causeway and took a large stretch with much effort. Here, Ixtlilxochitl killed another lord who was an enemy captain. He took back a sword that the captain had taken from a Spaniard whom he killed. On this day Alvarado wanted to enter the main square in Tlatelulco, which he set about to do with nearly fifty Spaniards. When they were inside the square, the enemy fell upon them. If Quauhtliztactzin had not arrived with his men, none of the Spaniards would have survived. Though Quauhtliztactzin hurried, he found that four Spaniards had already been captured by the enemy and sacrificed on the spot, right in front of them. They retreated as best they could, though it cost the lives of many native allies.

The next day Cortés moved the camp inside the city and did nothing else of importance. He ordered everyone, including the brigantines and the canoes, to charge from their positions on the following day. When the day dawned, he divided the people in his camp into three companies so that they could advance along three avenues that ran toward the square: along the first avenue went the treasurer, seventy Spanish foot soldiers, eight horses, and twenty thousand of Ixtlilxochitl's warriors, along with many sappers to fill canals and gaps and demolish houses; along the second avenue went Jorge de Alvarado and Andrés de Tapia with eighty Spaniards and more than twelve thousand allies given to them by Ixtlilxochitl, and at the entrance to this avenue they left two cannons, eight horsemen, and some allies; along the third avenue, Cortés and Ixtlilxochitl took one hundred Spaniards and eight thousand allies. When all were ready, they charged the enemy simultaneously and accomplished great things. In this assault, Ixtlilxochitl struck down another Mexica captain, cutting off both his legs with a single blow. Indeed they went along killing and taking houses, gaps, and barricades up to the square, leaving no survivors. It seemed that they would win Mexico that day.

The treasurer's men joined the advance to Tlatelulco, but they failed to fully fill a gap where the neighborhood of San Martín de Tlatelulco is today. Cortés, who followed them, advanced with his men, while Ixtlilxochitl remained behind fighting the Mexica. When Cortés arrived, having crossed the gap, he found the treasurer and others fleeing toward him. Many of the native allies had died. The standard-bearer had both of his arms cut off, and the royal banner fell into the hands of the enemy. As many as forty Spaniards were taken prisoner or killed.

Cortés, seeing the rage of the enemy, decided that it was better to flee. When they reached the gap, they were not able to cross it except by jumping in the water, and so they took one another's hands. Ixtlilxochitl, who got there just in time, ordered his soldiers to stop the enemy. He quickly reached Cortés and offered his hand and pulled him out of the water as one of the enemy warriors was about to cut off his head. Ixtlilxochitl cut off the attacker's arms. Though this is attributed to certain Spaniards, it is actually quite the opposite, since it could be seen painted on the main door of the monastery church at Santiago

Tlatelulco. But now a certain friar, who must have been one of Olea's relatives, had it repainted, making Olea the one to cut the arms of Cortés's attackers, while Ixtlilxochitl pulled him out of the water. In any case, Ixtlilxochitl saved Cortés and strongly reprimanded him because he had gone too far ahead and did not follow his advice never to go out on his own, but only in the company of many allies, so that the allies would be able to keep the enemy busy while the Spaniards could escape. There were only a few Spaniards, and if a single one of them died it was a greater loss than if five hundred natives died.

While Ixtlilxochitl was helping to pull Cortés from the water, he was hit over his left ear by a stone that almost fractured his skull. Seeing that he was injured, he took a little dirt and applied it to the wound. He took off the white armor that he always wore. Naked but for a buckler shield and a loincloth that covered his private parts, and enraged as he was, he charged the enemy with a *macana* and engaged them in a cruel battle, killing many of them until he met the brave general of the Mexica. The two fought for over a quarter of an hour, during which time the enemy shot an arrow that went through his right arm and a stone that hit him over his right knee. This hurt him, but not too much, and, in fact, only provoked him further. He took courage and charged the general, disarmed him, and wounded him in several places. Seeing himself defeated, the general fled as best he could. Ixtlilxochitl pursued him to the temple of the goddess Maquilxuchi, where he barricaded himself with his men so that Ixtlilxochitl could not capture him.

Ixtlilxochitl started back toward Cortés. On the way he met a Mexica captain coming toward him. Seeing that Ixtlilxochitl was attending to his wounds, the captain believed that Ixtlilxochitl could do him no harm and began to insult him and call him a thousand names. After ordering his men not to intervene, Ixtlilxochitl kept silent until he could suffer the insults no longer. Though his arm was wounded, he took the sword he had taken from the general and struck the captain across the waist and cut him in two. Unable to tolerate the arrow still stuck in his arm, he took it out and staunched the blood. His attendants applied certain remedies so that he healed after a few days.

Ixtlilxochitl reached Cortés on the Tlacopan causeway, where he was in retreat because the enemy had fallen upon him. They managed to return to their camp, having lost more than two thousand allies and forty Spaniards, who were sacrificed that day at the main temple in Tlatelulco, and another three who were burned. More than thirty were wounded. Many canoes were lost, and the brigantines were nearly lost. The captain and first mate of one of the brigantines were injured, and the captain died of his wounds. Four of Alvarado's men and some of his allies were also killed. This was an ill-fated day. All night long Cortés and Ixtlilxochitl and his men were very sad, and Cortés was also in pain because his leg was wounded. The Mexica, however, were joyful because of the notable victory they won on this day. They were so happy they stayed awake nearly all night celebrating and dancing, making bonfires on the rooftops of the temples and houses, playing their horns and drums, and exhibiting other signs of joy. Likewise, they opened up the canals and gaps as they had before. Quauhtemoc sent his ambassadors all around the district to spread the news of their success, especially in the provinces on their side, and to ask for reinforcements to win this war and oust the Spaniards from Mexico or kill them. The next day, to avoid appearing weak, Cortés and Ixtlilxochitl with their army went toward the city and fought the enemy up to the first gap before returning to their camp.

The second day after these unfortunate events, some ambassadors from Quauhnahuac came to tell Ixtlilxochitl that the people of Malinalco and Cuixco often attacked them. They asked him to order the neighboring towns to assist them. They also asked him to request from Cortés that some Spaniards go to support them. When Cortés heard this, he sent Andrés de Tapia with eighty foot soldiers and ten horsemen, giving them ten days to win those provinces and return to Mexico. Captain Tapia went with these messengers, and Ixtlilxochitl sent word to the neighboring towns to help. Nearly forty thousand men from Quauhnahuac marched with Andrés de Tapia on Malinalco. Before they got there, Tapia met the enemy army, fought against them, defeated them, killed many of them, and continued on to the city, which was very big. This done, they returned to Mexico.

Two days later some messengers from Toluca arrived to complain about their neighbors the Matlaltzinca, who had done them many wrongs and obstructed the aid that they were bringing in support of our forces. Cortés believed this because the Mexica had threatened that the Matlaltzinca, who were brave men, would come and destroy them. He ordered Sandoval to go with them and take with them eighteen horses, one hundred foot soldiers, and many allies that Ixtlil-xochitl sent to support them. Along with those who were in Toluca, there were nearly sixty thousand men. Sandoval traveled for three days, after which he crossed to the other side of the Chicuhnahuatl River. He caught up to the Matlaltzinca because they were carrying maize and other things they had taken from a place they had raided. They engaged them and fought for a while against them, until they made them flee and retreat to their city, which was more than two leagues away. During the retreat they killed more than two thousand Matlaltzinca. When they reached Malinalco, Sandoval's forces laid siege to it. The inhabitants fought back while the women climbed a tall hill. The combat lasted until, unable to resist any longer and seeing that their women and belongings were safe, the defenders fled. Our forces sacked the whole place, burned the houses and temples, and stayed to spend the night.

The next day they went to the hill and found no one. Then they came upon an enemy settlement, but the local lord opened the gates and welcomed our forces, begging them to do no harm in his land. He said he would make Matlaltzinco, Malinalco, Cohuizco, and other places on the side of the Mexica surrender. Sandoval was pleased and did him no harm but returned to Mexico. This lord brought those from Matlaltzinco, Malinalco, and the others to Cortés so that he would pardon them, offering him help for the siege of Mexico. Cortés was very pleased and asked them to be true to their word, and, indeed, they brought reinforcements, food, and other necessities.

While the conquests of Malinalco, Matlaltzinco, and other parts were going on, our forces did not do anything of note, though the natives would occasionally skirmish with the Mexica. Cortés, in agreement with Ixtlilxochitl and the other lords, ordered that all houses won should be razed to the ground. Ixtlilxochitl sent word to Tezcuco and the other kingdoms and provinces subject to his dominion, especially the ones nearby, for all the laborers to come quickly with their tools for this purpose. Four days after Sandoval returned to Mexico, more than one hundred thousand laborers arrived.

Meanwhile, the Mexica had thoroughly and deliberately prepared for the attack by placing stones on the square and streets so that the horses would not be able to run along them and other such tactics. After they had warned the Mexica to surrender, which they had not wanted to do by any means, Cortés, Ixtlilxochitl, and the rest began to fight on the main avenue leading to the main square. Our forces followed up the street, demolishing houses and filling up the gaps. Those in the city sued for peace—though it was an insincere gesture—which caused our forces to suspend the attack. When asked about the king, they answered that they had called for him.[57] They spent a while waiting for him to come, until the enemy began to throw stones, arrows, and spears. Our forces charged them and captured a great barricade that they had built.

They entered the square and used the stones to fill up the canal and the rest of the gaps on that street in such a way that the enemy was not able to open them up. They demolished as many houses as they could, and since it was time to go back to their camp, they left. For six days they busied themselves doing this—demolishing houses and fighting the enemy. During this time, while fighting the enemy, Ixtlilxochitl captured his brother Cohuanacoch, who was acting as general of the Mexica army, and delivered him to Cortés, who ordered him shackled and sent him to the camp under heavy guard. Quauhtemoc and the Mexica were very sorry to see this, because with the loss of this lord, they had lost all hope of any aid. Moreover, all of his Aculhua vassals who had been fighting on the side of Mexico went over to Ixtlilxochitl.

At this point Cortés staged an ambush in which they killed more than six hundred Mexica and caught more than two thousand, and the Mexica became increasingly frightened. Our forces were able to win many houses and a temple, in which the Spaniards found some gold in a tomb when the workers were demolishing it. On this day Ixtlilxochitl and the other lords and courageous soldiers of his army performed great and notable deeds as they had before, which are not mentioned to avoid verbosity.

The next night two starving Mexica came to Ixtlilxochitl, who was pleased to see them. From them he got news about everything that was going on inside the city, the difficulties, hunger, and pestilence afflicting the citizens; how by night and at unusual hours they came out to fish and to scavenge for wild plants and tree bark to

---

57. King Cuauhtemoc. Cortés's "Third Letter" mentions several junctures at which he unsuccessfully requested an audience with the Mexica leader. Commenting on Mexico's defeat, Gómara (1979, 277) reasoned that by the end the people were in such miserable condition that they would have sued for peace, but that Cuauhtemoc adamantly refused.

sustain themselves. When Ixtlilxochitl heard about this, knowing the places where the Mexica foraged, he informed Cortés. Brigantines and canoes were sent to surround the city. They posted lookouts to determine when they came out of the city. Cortés took nearly one hundred Spaniards and fifteen horsemen, and Ixtlilxochitl nearly forty thousand men. Early one morning, after being advised by the lookouts, they fell upon the unfortunate Mexica and, since they were unarmed, killed almost one thousand of them and captured many others. The brigantines and the canoes did the same. Even though the city guards raised the alarm and signaled that they wanted to engage our forces, the Mexica did not dare fight.

The next day was the second of the week called *ome malinalli*, 2 Grass, which was on the tenth day of the month called *huey tecu-hylhuitl*,[58] and in our calendar July 24, eve of the feast day of Saint James, the patron saint of Spain. With their army Cortés and Ixtlil-xochitl fought the city, took control of the whole Tlacopan causeway, and destroyed and burned down King Quauhtemoc's palaces and many other houses. On this day three of the four parts of Mexico were won. Therefore, our forces could communicate without danger, those from Cortés and Ixtlilxochitl's camp with those from Alvarado and Tetlahuehuezquititzin's. Four days after they had burned many houses and toppled the walls, our forces won two large temples in Tlatelulco, where their greatest forces were located, though it took some effort. Seeing that the enemy would not fight after the temples had been taken, Ixtlilxochitl told them to surrender to the Christians, which would be to their benefit. The enemy fighters told them not to speak of friendship nor to expect any spoils from them because they were going to burn all that they had and throw it in the water, as they had done with the treasure, where it would never be found again. And they said that if a single one of them remained, he would die defending his homeland. Hearing this, Ixtlilxochitl informed Cortés. He told him that he should not expect any peace agreement, but that he should continue his pursuit.

For four days they did not battle with the Mexica—some say that they were busy working on a catapult—and after those days they entered the city to fight again. They found the streets full of women,

---

58. The Great Festival of the Lords was celebrated in the eighth month of the Nahua solar calendar (Aguilar-Moreno 2006, 296).

children, and elderly, and many others who were sick and starving. Cortés and Ixtlilxochitl ordered their men not to harm them. The nobles and the soldiers were on the rooftops without any weapons because it was the beginning of their month called *micaylhuitzintli*,[59] a feast day that they observed and that usually falls on August 7. When they were asked to surrender, they replied that they would deal with this another day, since they were celebrating the feast of their deceased children. In light of this, Cortés and Ixtlilxochitl sent word to Alvarado and Tetlahuehuezquititzin to attack a well-fortified neighborhood that had more than a thousand houses and had not yet been captured. They said they would help. And so they attacked this neighborhood, and the inhabitants fought formidably for a long time. Not being able to resist the zeal of our forces, they fled and abandoned their houses. More than twelve or thirteen thousand men were killed. On this day the Spaniards almost did not fight at all except at the beginning, and then they moved to one side and watched their allies as they fought. On this occasion, Ixtlilxochitl personally captured almost one hundred men and killed many others, among them twenty captains who were later recognized by the armor they were wearing.

Quauhtemoc was in this neighborhood, which was the last to fall. There were so few houses and so many people that there was hardly room to stand. The streets were filled with corpses and sick men, so our forces had to walk on their bodies. The next day they fought over what was left of the city, maybe one part out of eight. As they were fighting, they called Cortés and Ixtlilxochitl and spoke many emotional words, asking them to finish them off. They addressed Cortés in particular, speaking those words that the Spanish chroniclers relate: "Oh, Captain Cortés, since you are the son of the sun, why don't you tell him to destroy us, etc." Out of pity they did not kill anyone that day, except for some who were trying to defend themselves.

The next day Cortés and Ixtlilxochitl sent his mother's brother, who had been captured by Ixtlilxochitl two days before and was still wounded, to Quauhtemoc, asking him to bid for peace. His uncle tried to excuse himself, explaining to his nephew the will of the king. But he went, nonetheless. The guards let him in, welcoming him as

59. Little Festival of the Dead.

their lord. Once he delivered his message, their only response was to sacrifice him. The Spaniards and natives who had gone with him were thrown out amid a flurry of stones and spear points, and the Mexica shouted that they would rather die than surrender. On this day there was much fighting, and many people died on both sides.

The next day our forces returned to the enemy's position and did not fight, waiting to see if the Mexica would surrender. Cortés and Ixtlilxochitl approached a barricade, where Ixtlilxochitl talked to some of his kinsmen. He told them what was best for them. They replied that they were well aware of their predicament but that they were bound to obey their king. They discussed this and other things; the Mexica lords responded with many tears. After he told them to go beg their king to give himself up, they went and asked him over and over to do this. But he repeatedly answered that this should have been done earlier, because now all was lost. They returned to Ixtlilxochitl and told him that the king could not come to meet him and Cortés, because it was already late, but that the next day around lunch time he would surely come to the square to speak with them. Meanwhile, our forces returned to their camp very satisfied, believing that this time they would reach an agreement.

The next day, early in the morning, they had a stage set up on the square where they would discuss the surrender and eat together. When the time came, the king did not show up, but rather five lords, including the governor and captain general,[60] arrived to discuss the terms of their surrender. They excused their king, who was sick. Cortés welcomed them and was pleased to see them. He entertained them, but by no means did he want to negotiate with them. He told them that without the king no agreement could be reached. They went to their king, who told them that it would be a great disgrace for a king like him to go before his enemies except in battle to take their life. He told them to go back and tell Ixtlilxochitl to tell Cortés that he gave his word that he would comply with whatever his ambassadors agreed to, since they were the greatest lords in his kingdom. But there was no way he could go before Cortés. If this was not enough, then they should do as they wished; they had all but defeated them already. Ixtlilxochitl related to Cortés everything that

60. Gómara (1979, 276) identifies this man as the *cihuacoatl*, who was the senior adviser to the Mexica ruler.

was happening and told him what King Quauhtemoc had said. Cortés
sent word to him once again that the following day he would go to
the square for the last time, and he would wait for him there for up
to three hours. If Quauhtemoc did not come to meet them, then they
would destroy them without mercy. The messengers returned and
informed their king of Cortés's decision.

The next day, which was the sixth day called *macuili toxtli*,
5 Rabbit, of their eighth month called *micaylhuitzintli*, and according to our calendar August 12, the feast day of Saint Clare, Cortés
went with Ixtlilxochitl and other lords to the square to wait for King
Quauhtemoc, as they had agreed. They were there from the early
morning until almost noon, waiting for King Quauhtemoc. Seeing
that he did not come and losing hope that he would, they sent Sandoval and the lords that were with him along with the brigantines and
the canoes to engage the enemy on the canals and the lake. Cortés
and Ixtlilxochitl fought in the streets and at the barricades. The battle
began, but after a short while our forces penetrated the strongest
Mexica defenses, meeting little resistance. Fifty thousand men were
killed or captured.

On this day some of the cruelest things ever to occur in these
lands were inflicted upon the unfortunate Mexica. The wailing of
the women and children was such that it broke the men's hearts.
The Tlaxcalteca and other nations that were not on good terms with
the Mexica cruelly took revenge on them for past deeds and plundered everything they had. Ixtlilxochitl and his men pitied them
and prevented the others from treating the women and the children
with such cruelty, since, after all, the Mexica were his compatriots
and many of them his kinsmen. Cortés and the Spaniards also took
pity on them. As night was falling they retired to their camp. On this
night Cortés, Ixtlilxochitl, and the rest of the captains decided that
the next day they would win what was left of the city.

The next day, on the feast day of Saint Hippolytus, they went
toward the last bastion of the enemy. Cortés went through the
streets, and Ixtlilxochitl with Sandoval, as the captain of the brigantines, went by water toward an inlet, since Ixtlilxochitl had been
informed that King Quauhtemoc was there with many people on
boats. They approached them, and it was an extraordinary sight to
see the Mexica: the warriors, sad and confused, near the edge of the
rooftops witnessing their ruin; the children, elderly, and women

wailing; the lords and the nobles in the canoes with their king, all of them dazed. Once the signal was given, our forces charged the enemy bastion all at once. The assault proceeded so quickly that in a few hours they won, and nothing was left to the enemy. The brigantines and canoes charged those of the enemy, and since the Mexica could not resist, they fled as best they could while our forces chased them down. Garciholguín, the captain of the brigantine, who had been informed by a Mexica whom he held prisoner that King Quauhtemoc was in the canoe they were following, went after it and caught up with it. King Quauhtemoc, seeing that his enemies were near, ordered the rowers to move closer to them in order to fight and took up his shield and *macana*. But then he recognized the superiority of the enemy, who threatened him with their crossbows and guns, and he surrendered.

Garciholguín took him to Cortés, who received him courteously because, after all, he was a king. Quauhtemoc grabbed Cortés's dagger and said, "Oh, captain. I have done everything in my power to defend my kingdom and save it from you, but since I have been unfortunate, take my life. This would be just, and so doing you will finish off the Mexica kingdom, since you have already destroyed my city and killed my vassals." Quauhtemoc made other woeful declarations, which moved everyone present. Cortés consoled him and asked him to order his men to give themselves up, which he did. Quauhtemoc climbed a high tower and in a loud voice ordered them to surrender, since he was now in the hands of his enemies. No more than sixty thousand warriors remained out of the three hundred thousand that fought for Mexico; upon seeing their king, they dropped their weapons. The highest-ranking nobles arrived to console their king.

Ixtlilxochitl had been eager to capture Quauhtemoc himself, but he was not able to do so since he was in a canoe, which is not as fast as a brigantine. He was able to reach only two other canoes, in which he found some princes and lords such as Tetlepanquetzal, heir to the kingdom of Tlacopan; and Tlacahuepantzin, Moteczuma's son and heir; along with many others. In the other canoe was Queen Papantzin Oxocotzin, Quauhtemoc's legitimate wife who had previously been married to King Quitlahuac, along with many ladies. Ixtlilxochitl seized them, taking these lords to Cortés while he ordered the queen and other ladies be taken under heavy guard to be held in the city of Tezcuco.

According to the histories, paintings, and accounts, especially the one by don Alonso Axayaca, the siege of Mexico lasted a full eighty days, and 30,000 of Ixtlilxochitl's Tezcuca warriors died, besides the 200,000 that were fighting alongside the Spaniards, as we have seen. On the Mexica side, more than 240,000 men died, among them nearly all the Mexica nobility. Only a few lords and gentlemen remained, most of them young children. This day, after having sacked the city, the Spaniards took the gold and silver for themselves, while the lords took the jewels and precious feathers. The soldiers took the blankets and everything else. Then they spent another four days burying the dead and in joyful celebration. They took many men and women as slaves. Then they went to Culhuacan with the whole army, where all the lords said good-bye to Ixtlilxochitl and went back to their lands, promising to support him in all his endeavors. Cortés thanked them profusely. The Tlaxcalteca, Huexotzinca, and Cho-lulteca said good-bye to him and likewise went back to their lands, wealthy and content. On the way the Tlaxcalteca plundered the city of Tezcuco and other places, stealing at night when the inhabitants could not hear them or protect their belongings from them.

Afterward, the Spaniards settled in Coyohuacan. They were cared for and entertained by the Aculhua, who had been ordered by Ixtlilxochitl to provide everything they needed. Ixtlilxochitl returned to his city of Tezcuco, where he was welcomed. He found the entire city sacked and ruined by the Tlaxcalteca. He had everything cleaned and repaired, especially the palaces of his father and grandfather and those of other lords. He sent a message to Tlaxcala reprimanding them for the way they had abused the city of Tezcuco, the ancient homeland from which the Tlaxcalteca ancestors had come. The Tlax-calteca apologized halfheartedly, saying they were not to blame. They said the Spaniards forced them and made many other excuses. Ixtlil-xochitl gave out many rewards to all the lords, captains, and soldiers who fought in his army in support of the Christians, especially those who distinguished themselves in battle.

Ixtlilxochitl ordered the Mexica whom he brought from Mexico— he had personally captured almost two thousand of them—to build great houses and palaces at the place called Tecpilpan. His father had given him the town as a child, and he grew up there. He ordered all his vassals there to always be prepared with everything they might need in case of war or emergency. Cortés, who was in Coyohuacan, realized that all the treasure from the three capitals that he had seen in Mexico was missing. So he ordered a lord who was in the service of Quauhtemoc burned alive and King Quauhtemoc himself to be tortured by having his feet burned. He did this in spite of the fact that the Mexica told Cortés that even if he killed every single one of them, he would never find the treasure because they had thrown it in the middle of the lake. Ixtlilxochitl could not abide Cortés's cruelty. He asked that Cortés stop torturing King Quauhtemoc, because Ixtlilxochitl knew that it was futile and inhumane and would provide an excuse for the Mexica to take up arms again. Recognizing his cruelty and the risk it represented, Cortés ordered the king released.

Cohuanacoch, whose legs were gravely injured from the shackles he had been wearing since he was captured by his brother, begged Ixtlilxochitl to be released. Ixtlilxochitl asked Cortés to be kind enough to remove his brother's shackles, because his feet were injured and he had been punished enough. Cortés replied that he could not free him until he received orders from the Spanish emperor; Cortés had sent word of everything that was happening to His Majesty on the fleet that took the royal fifth,[61] and he would soon receive a reply. Cortés said that if Cohuanacoch was so gravely injured, that Ixtlilxochitl should send some gold from Tezcuco to ransom him; the gold would be sent to the emperor, who would appreciate the gesture. Ixtlilxochitl replied that if it was only a matter of gold, he preferred his brother's health to all the treasures in the world. And so he sent to Tezcuco for the gold that remained in his father's and grandfather's palaces and all the gold that was in his own houses. He gave all this to Cortés, who said that it was not enough to ransom a great lord such as his brother and that more was needed. Again Ixtlilxochitl sent word to all the lords—his cousins, brothers, and kinsmen—who had houses in the city, and they gathered all of their jewels and pieces of gold. Once they gathered the gold and silver from four hundred lordly houses in the city, they sent it to Ixtlilxochitl, who gave it to Cortés. He ransomed his brother and sent him to Tezcuco, where his vassals tearfully received him when they saw how sick, emaciated, and abused he was. They nursed him back to health.

61. The "royal fifth" was a 20 percent tax levied on all plunder, spoils, and resources extracted from the Indies.

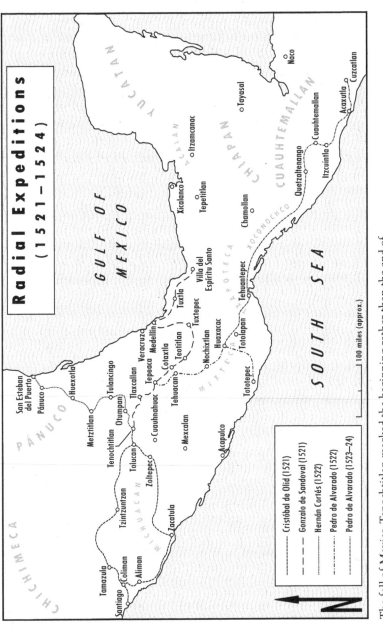

The fall of Mexico-Tenochtitlan marked the beginning rather than the end of the conquest of New Spain. Map by Pablo García.

Meanwhile, the king of Mixhuacan[62] named Catzontzin, having heard of Mexico's defeat and fearing that the Christians and allies would march on his kingdom, sent ambassadors to congratulate Cortés. He offered his service to the emperor and his alliance and also to Ixtlilxochitl for his aid to Cortés, thanking him for everything he had done in support of the Christians. He offered his condolences to the Mexica lords and those on their side for their travails and mistreatment. This delegation included a brother of the king, who was accompanied by a thousand men. Everyone was pleased with the delegation and the peace with Mixhuacan. The Aculhua were relieved not to have to undertake the conquest of Mixhuacan, which was a large and bellicose kingdom. Cortés sent Cristóbal de Olid with one hundred foot soldiers and forty horsemen, and Ixtlilxochitl sent more than five thousand men to serve and assist. When they arrived in Mixhuacan in the city of Chinzizilan,[63] which was the capital of the kingdom, Catzontzin received them and was pleased to see the Christians and have them settle in the city, which they did. He promised to be an ally of the Spaniards, the Aculhua, and all their would-be allies from then on.

After King Cacama had been captured and killed, the provinces and kingdoms subject to Tezcuco that lie on the coast of both the North and the South Seas[64] rebelled against the Spaniards. They killed all the Spaniards whom they found in their lands looking for gold and trading with the natives. Even though Tecocoltzin and Ixtlilxochitl sent messages demanding that they surrender to the Spaniards and support them in the wars with Mexico, they never complied. And so Cortés and Ixtlilxochitl agreed to send warriors to subdue them. They had been in Coyohuacan a little over two months when Cortés sent Gonzalo de Sandoval to Cohuatzacualco, Toxtepec, Huatoxco,[65] and other regions, with two hundred Spaniards on foot and five on horseback. Ixtlilxochitl sent thirty thousand warriors

62. Michoacan. Located to the west of the Mexico Basin, this Purepecha-speaking region was politically independent of the Triple Alliance and led by a ruler known as the *calzonzi*. On the conquest of Michoacan, see Warren (1985).

63. Tzintzuntzan.

64. The Atlantic Ocean was also called the North Sea, and the Pacific was also known as the South Sea.

65. These places are all located to the southeast of Mexico City, near the Gulf of Mexico.

with them, which included veterans, kinsmen, and vassals; he sent some of his brothers and some lords as their captains. When they reached Huatoxco, the Aculhua general sent word to those in this province to surrender, unless they wanted war. The people in the province surrendered.

Then they went to Toxtepec, which is 120 leagues from Mexico and one of Tezcuco's subject provinces. Toxtepec also surrendered; the Spaniards settled here and called it Medellín. From here they marched on Cohuatzacualco, where they met some resistance, because the natives of this province would not surrender. One night they conquered a place in this province, where they captured a noblewoman, which caused the whole province to surrender to our forces. The province was made up of many towns that were on the banks of the Cohuatzacualco River. About four leagues from the sea, Sandoval established the Villa del Espíritu Santo, where some Aculhua stayed with the Spanish settlers, as they had done in other places. The Aculhua captains sent messages on behalf of Ixtlilxochitl to the provinces of Quecholan, Zihuatlan, Quetzaltepec, Tabaxco, and many other towns and places subject to Tezcuco, Mexico, and Tlacopan, demanding that they surrender and ally themselves with the Spaniards, which they did. The lords of these provinces came to the Villa del Espíritu Santo, where they negotiated their surrender with the Tezcuca general and Sandoval; they paid two years' worth of tribute that they owed to Tezcuco.

At the same time, Ixtlilxochitl sent some warriors to support those in Tepeaca, Itzucan, and other cities subject to Tezcuco, whose neighbors, the kingdoms of the Mixteca, Zapoteca, and Huaxacac,[66] did them great harm. They had three battles on separate occasions, because they were very belligerent people. Many died on both sides, but they eventually managed to subdue Huaxacac and a great part of the Mixteca.

Ixtlilxochitl sent some messengers to Tequantepec, Zacatulan, and other provinces that were in rebellion against Tezcuco and the Spaniards. Four Spaniards went with them along two different routes; Cortés had sent them to scout the South Sea. When they reached these parts, the lords and all their people sent their apologies to Ixtlilxochitl for failing to obey and to the Spaniards for not

66. Oaxaca.

having supported them. They brought the tribute that they had failed to send for two years. Tototepec alone would not surrender, and they were angry at the others for allying themselves with Ixtlilxochitl and the Spaniards. They sent word to Ixtlilxochitl to send reinforcements to help subdue Tototepec and to ask Cortés to send some Christians to aid them. Having been fully informed about the South Sea by the four Spaniards who had gone with Ixtlilxochitl's messengers, Cortés sent Pedro de Alvarado to aid the lord of Tequantepec and the others who were on our side. He sent two hundred Spaniards and forty horsemen; Ixtlilxochitl sent twenty thousand warriors along with them.

In the year 1522 they marched on Tototepec, and it took them one month to subdue it. On the journey through Huaxacac, they found some resistance. When they arrived in Tototepec, the Aculhua general asked the lord and his whole province to surrender. The lord of Tototepec agreed, though insincerely, and he welcomed our forces. He wanted to take them to some great houses he had in order to lodge them. The Aculhua told Alvarado not to accept the invitation, because they had been warned that that night they would set fire to the houses, which were covered in straw. Alvarado followed the advice, and they set up camp on the outskirts of the city. Alvarado seized the lord and his son. Seeing themselves apprehended and their treason discovered, they ransomed themselves with more than twenty five thousand gold *castellanos*.[67] They settled in this city and province and sent demands for surrender to those in the provinces of Coaztlahuac, Tlaxquiauhco, and other parts that had also rebelled. They all quickly surrendered, and with that, the Aculhua returned to Tezcuco and Alvarado to Coyohuacan, where they recounted all that they had done on this journey.

Seeing that those on the South Sea coast were allies, Cortés decided to send forty Spanish carpenters and sailors to Zacatulan to build two brigantines to be used to explore all of the coast and two caravels to look for islands, since he had news of some that were very rich. For this purpose he asked Ixtlilxochitl to provide some carpenters and some people to carry the iron, mooring ropes, sails, lanyards, and rigging from ships in Veracruz. Ixtlilxochitl did all this without

67. A type of coin used in Castile.

hesitation; he sent his vassals to assist the Spaniards with everything they should ask for or need.

Cortés and Ixtlilxochitl were told that Cristóbal de Olid was defeated by the people of Coliman, who killed ten Spaniards and many people from Mixhuacan, who were on their side. By order of Cortés, Olid was on his way from Mixhuacan to Zacatulan to see the brigantines, with more than one hundred Spaniards, forty horsemen, and many Mixhuacan natives. He tried to take Coliman on the way, but it did not go well for him, as has been said. And so Cortés quickly sent Gonzalo de Sandoval with sixty foot soldiers and twenty-five horsemen, and Ixtlilxochitl sent with them sixteen thousand warriors to take revenge on and punish those from Coliman. At the same time, they were to punish the people of Impiltzinco, who made war on their neighbors for having been the Spaniards' allies and on the side of Ixtlilxochitl. Sandoval and the Aculhua went straight to Impiltzinco. They marched on this province, but they were never able to defeat them because the people were very belligerent and the land was rough. And so they moved on to Zacatulan, where they gathered more people and marched on Coliman, which lies sixty leagues from Zacatulan. Once there, they fought a cruel battle. Many enemies but only some Aculhua died. The surviving enemies, seeing themselves hard-pressed by our forces, surrendered, along with those from Impiltzinco, Zihuatlan, Colimatlec, and other towns. After having settled these provinces and Coliman, our forces returned.

Meanwhile, Ixtlilxochitl was busy rebuilding Mexico with more than four hundred thousand men—skilled craftsmen, carpenters, stonecutters, masons, and their laborers. Ixtlilxochitl was living in Tlatelulco, from where he dispatched his captains for the expeditions and governed all the land, especially the Aculhua territories. Ixtlilxochitl and the other lords agreed that Mexico should be rebuilt, because it was the city where the Christians had met the most resistance, and the Aculhua had won it with much effort and bloodshed. The rebuilt city would commemorate for all time the glorious victory they had won against Mexico. The houses that were built, which were better than the ones that had been there, numbered over one hundred thousand, forty thousand more than before. When the city was divided among the lords, Ixtlilxochitl received Tlatelulco, and he built some houses. The rest of the lords each received a neighborhood. Tlacahuepantzin, the son of Moteczuma, who was called don Pedro, received the neighborhood of Atzaqualco.

As soon as Cortés won Mexico he sent word to our lord the emperor of all that he had done and asked him to send missionaries for the conversion of the natives. His Majesty sent word to Cortés that he would inform His Holiness[68] and send some with his permission. At this time he sent only five or six Franciscan friars, among them Father fray Pedro de Gante, His Majesty's cousin; and another four clerics. The emperor expressed his satisfaction with what Cortés had done. These friars arrived in the year 1522, right after Ixtlilxochitl had finished rebuilding Mexico.

Acting on behalf of the emperor, Cortés told Ixtlilxochitl that he would give him and his descendants three provinces: Otumpan, with thirty-three towns; Itziuhcohuac, with just as many and which lies near Pánuco; and Cholula, with a number of towns. Ixtlilxochitl responded by saying that what Cortés was offering was already his and had always belonged to his family; it had not been taken away, and it was not the emperor's to give. Ixtlilxochitl told Cortés that he was welcome to enjoy these lands, since the Spaniards had toiled so much and traveled so many leagues by land and sea, putting their lives at great risk. As it stood, the inhabitants of those provinces and the rest of those in his kingdom of Tezcuco were Ixtlilxochitl's vassals and would be loyal to him and his brothers as their natural lords. Having heard this, Cortés saw that these arguments were true and was quiet and did not insist.

Ixtlilxochitl went to Tezcuco, where he and his brother Cohuanacoch agreed to split the kingdom of Tezcuco in this way: Cohuanacoch, as lord, would stay in the city of Tezcuco and take all the southern provinces, which are Chalco, Quaunahuac, Iztzocan, Tlahuic, and all the others on the way to the South Sea; Ixtlilxochitl took the northern half and placed boundary markers at Tepetlaoztoc, Papaluca, Tenayucan, Chicuanauhtla, and Xaltocan, making Otumpan and Teotihuacan his capitals. He took for himself Tolantzinco, Teziuhcohacac, Tlatlauhquitepec, Pahuatla, and all the rest up to the North Sea and Pánuco. Once the agreement had been made, Ixtlilxochitl went to Otumpan, where he built some palaces. He did the same

---

68. Pope Leo X.

in Teotihuacan, where he arrived the last day of the year of *nahui toxtli,*[69] which according to our calendar was March 19, 1523.

After having seen King Quauhtemoc tortured, the Mexica lords who had escaped the wars in Mexico revolted and rose up against Cortés again, as Ixtlilxochitl had warned they would do. In time Ixtlilxochitl put down the rebellion. The leaders were caught, and many of them were sentenced to death. Some were hanged and others were thrown to the dogs to be torn to pieces. One of these was Cohuanacoch, which caused Ixtlilxochitl to get very angry with Cortés. Going against the Spaniards, Ixtlilxochitl had his brother rescued from the dogs that were about to tear him apart.

While Mexico was being rebuilt, Cortés and Ixtlilxochitl marched against the kingdom of Pánuco, some parts of which had rebelled against Tezcuco. Moreover, the people of Pánuco had killed a number of Spaniards and committed other insults and offenses against our people. Cortés took 300 Spaniards on foot and 150 horsemen, while Ixtlilxochitl took more than 40,000 Aculhua and some Mexica. They arrived in Ayutuxtitlan, where the enemy came out to attack them, and in a flat and barren field, they had a cruel battle. Being on the front lines, over 5,000 of Ixtlilxochitl's men died. More than 15,000 enemy warriors perished, and 50 Spaniards were wounded. They spent four days here resting, and the subjects of Tezcuco who were in rebellion came to surrender and brought all the tribute that they had not given in years past. Ixtlilxochitl forgave them and then went to Chila, which is near the sea, where Francisco de Garay had been defeated.[70]

When they reached this place, Ixtlilxochitl sent his messengers all over the region, demanding that the people surrender to the Spaniards. Trusting in their courage and their fortified positions, they never wanted to surrender. Cortés and Ixtlilxochitl waited for fifteen days to see if the people of Chila would surrender. Not only did they refuse to surrender, but they killed Ixtlilxochitl's messengers. Cortés and Ixtlilxochitl, therefore, decided to wage war against them. They were not able to defeat them because they had taken refuge on the lakes. One night, after having found some canoes, Cortés

---

69. 4 Rabbit.

70. Francisco de Garay made two expeditions to Pánuco from Cuba, the first in 1519 and the second in 1523; neither was successful.

and Ixtlilxochitl crossed to the other side of the river without being noticed. Cortés had 100 foot soldiers and 40 horsemen, while Ixtlil-xochitl had nearly 20,000. As the sun rose, the enemy saw them and attacked them. They were almost defeated and our forces destroyed, but they fought so skillfully that they defeated the enemy. They pursued them for over a league; a great number of them died, and 10,000 of Ixtlilxochitl's men were wounded.

That night they slept in a deserted town and found in the temples the skins of the Spaniards who had been with Garay, whom they had flayed; their clothes and weapons hung on the walls. From this it is clear that the first Spaniards, who came to these parts without allies, were unsuccessful and met with disaster. It was exactly the opposite in the case of Cortés. Whenever he went to conquer or fight some province, he was always victorious because he had allies. They were the ones who took the lead and were the first to take the risks.

After they spent the night in this place, they went to another very beautiful and fertile place, where many armed enemy fighters conspired to catch them by surprise from inside the houses. Our forces were aware of this. Realizing that they had been seen, the enemy came out to fight against our forces. On this day they had a great battle in which many of them died. Some of ours died, and many Spaniards were wounded. The enemy was defeated three times on this day, but they regrouped just as many times. When they finally grew tired, they jumped into a nearby river and crossed to the other side, remaining on the bank and on guard until dark. Our forces turned back. Ixtlilxochitl and his men ate some wild plants and berries, while Cortés and his men ate a horse. They slept under heavy guard.

The next day they marched on four towns that were all abandoned, and they slept in some maize fields, where they satisfied their hunger. They went on for another two days, and since they found no one, they returned to their camp in Chila. The following night, after they got to Chila, they staged an attack on a large town on the lakeshore both by water and by land and plundered all the houses. The inhabitants quickly surrendered, and twenty-five days later the rest of the people in that district and the people along the river surrendered. In a place near Chila, Cortés established a town he called Santiesteban del Puerto, where he stationed some Spaniards; Ixtlilxochitl ordered some of his vassals to stay with them. Cortés and Ixtlil-xochitl decimated Pánuco, Chila, and other big settlements to avenge the cruelties committed against Garay's men. Once this was done, they turned back to Mexico. Then, Tototepec del Norte, with another twenty-some towns subject to the city of Tezcuco, rebelled in quick succession. They pillaged and burned more than twenty towns in the province and the kingdom of Tezcuco, and Cortés and Ixtlilxochitl had no choice but to attack them. Taking more than thirty thousand warriors, they fought against them. Ixtlilxochitl personally captured the general and lord of Tototepec and delivered him to Cortés, who had him hanged. Many people died on both sides, and those who were captured were sold into slavery. Ixtlilxochitl made the brother of the previous ruler the lord of Tototepec.

The Spaniards who had been in Pánuco, especially some who had been with Garay, were so cruel to those of Pánuco that they had no choice but to rebel, because they could not endure it. They killed over four hundred Spaniards. When Cortés found out about this, he asked for reinforcements from Ixtlilxochitl and Quauhtemoc, whose vassals had nursed him back to health. Each of them contributed more than fifteen thousand warriors. Cortés sent them along with Gonzalo de Sandoval, fifty Spaniards on horse, and one hundred on foot to Pánuco. Yoyontzin, Ixtlilxochitl's younger brother, went as the general of the Aculhua, and Quauhtemoc's nephew led the Mexica. When they reached Pánuco they fought and defeated the enemy twice. When they finally reached Santiesteban, they found only one hundred Spaniards; if they had delayed only one more day they would have found none.

They divided up into three companies and went inland, killing, plundering, and burning all the houses. Within a few days, they sacked everything, and they killed an infinite number of Indians. Our forces captured the lords of sixty towns, four hundred nobles and captains, and a lot of commoners. The lords and the captains were sentenced to death and were burned, and the common people were released. At this execution, the lords' own children were present, especially their heirs, so that they would learn a lesson. Then their dominions and titles were returned to them. In this way Pánuco was pacified, and our forces returned to Mexico.

In 1523 Ixtlilxochitl and Quauhtemoc learned that the people in Quauhtemalan,[71] Otlatlan, Chiapan, Xoconuxco, and other provinces

71. Guatemala.

in the south that were subject to the three capitals[72] had recently rebelled. They attacked the people who were on the side of the Christians, who were their mortal enemies because they had insulted and aggrieved them. Cortés was informed. He had already planned to send some Spaniards to explore the land. Seeing that it was first necessary to conquer these territories, he told the lords to send their vassals with Alvarado for this purpose. Quauhtemoc and Ixtlilxochitl, who had readied their vassals, gathered twenty thousand experienced warriors who were knowledgeable about the terrain. Each one sent a general with ten thousand warriors to go with Alvarado, who took more than three hundred Spaniards.

They left Mexico on December 6. They went by way of Tequantepec to Xoconuxco. On the way they punished many cities and towns that were in rebellion, especially Tzapotolan, a large and well-fortified city, where they fought for many days. Many people died on both sides. Many Spaniards were wounded, and Tzapotolan was defeated. They went on to Quetzaltenanco, spending three days on the road. On the first they crossed two rivers with difficulty. On the second they climbed a rough, steep slope for five leagues, and at an especially steep point they encountered four thousand enemy fighters and fought them until they defeated them. Farther along, as the terrain leveled out, they found more than thirty thousand enemy warriors, against whom they fought. And even farther along, near certain mountain springs, they fought again, but quickly won. The enemy regrouped on the lower slopes of the mountain and turned again on our forces with more vigor. They fought a fierce battle, but soon our forces defeated them and pursued them. In the pursuit they killed an infinite number of enemies and captured the general, one of the four lords that ruled Otlatlan at that time. Many of our men died, as well as some Spaniards.

The following day they reached Quetzaltenanco and found no one. There they supplied themselves with food and other necessities. Six days after they had left Tzapotolan and had traveled a great distance, the people of Quetzaltenanco joined together and fell on our forces. They came to meet them and fought very well. Those from Quetzaltenanco, having experienced the rage of our forces, retreated. During the pursuit, our forces killed a great number of them, especially as

---

72. Mexico, Tetzcoco, and Tlacopan.

they attempted to ford a stream. The captains and lords retreated to a hill, where they were captured and killed. Realizing they had been defeated, the lords of Otlatlan and Quetzaltenanco brought their neighbors together and talked about jointly feigning surrender. They gave many blankets, gold, and other things to their new allies. Once they had established their alliance, they invited our forces to go to Otlatlan, where they would be welcomed. Our forces went there and found signs of the ambush that those in Otlatlan had prepared. They withdrew and suffered some injuries, but not before they skillfully managed to capture the enemy lords. This angered their vassals. As a result, they fought with more fury and nearly surrounded our forces. Many Aculhua, Mexica, and even Spaniards died each day. Seeing this, Alvarado ordered the captured lords to be burned with the utmost cruelty. The generals of Tezcuco and Mexico sent word to Quauhtemalan asking for aid. The lord there sent them more than four thousand warriors to fight their enemies. They fought with such urgency that they defeated them. The citizens asked to be pardoned and shown mercy, which was granted. The children of the two lords of Otlatlan and Quetzaltenanco who had been burned were released, and they promised never to rebel again.

After having conquered Otlatlan and Quetzaltenanco, they went with the whole army to Quauhtemalan, where they were welcomed with much rejoicing and celebrating. The lords apologized to the generals for not having gone to Mexico with their tribute. They blamed the Spaniards who were in their land and had insulted and aggrieved them. There was a large province near Quauhtemalan that often fought against this city and Otlatlan and others that were on the side of the three capitals. This province had its capital city on the shore of a large lake. It was well fortified and heavily populated. Our forces sent word demanding surrender, but they wanted nothing but war. So our forces, along with many from Quauhtemalan, attacked them and fought until they had taken their hill and plundered their houses. Some were able to cross over to a small island in canoes or by swimming, and they escaped. Our forces left the hill for some cultivated fields, where they set up camp and spent the night. The next day they entered the city and found it abandoned. Since the people had lost the hill, which was their fortress, they left the city.

Our forces traveled around the land and captured some men, three or four of whom were sent to ask their lords to surrender. If they did so, they would be well treated; if they did not, their houses and lands would be destroyed. They replied that they wanted peace, and they surrendered. This province had never been dominated by any other nation. Alvarado and the rest returned to Quauhtemalan, where many towns that were in rebellion came to surrender, including those on the southern coast. Those from the province of Ixquintepec were in rebellion, and they attacked all who came to see the Christians. Our army marched on them, and they walked for four days, sleeping always out in the open. On the fourth day they entered the outskirts of the city without being seen or heard. It was raining; the inhabitants of the city were in their houses and not paying attention. They attacked them while they were inside the houses. They caught and killed many of them. Since the inhabitants could not muster a defense, most of them fled. The rest of them gathered and barricaded themselves into some large houses. They fought against and killed many natives of Tezcuco, Mexico, and Quautemalan and wounded some Spaniards. Our forces set fire to the town. The lord, seeing his ruin, came and asked them to have mercy on him and negotiated his surrender with our forces. They spent eight days resting, and during this time all the towns subject to this province surrendered, offering their alliance and service.[73]

From here they went to other provinces that had never been subject to the three capitals and where they spoke different languages. The first place they reached was Caltipar, and they defeated them. Then they went to Tatixco and then to Necendelan, where they had a number of battles with the natives of these provinces, and some of our forces died. They were robbed as they traveled along the road, and almost all the plunder they were carrying was stolen. They never managed to make an alliance in this region and so continued on to Pazuco, where the people pretended to be friendly, but only to put our forces at ease and kill them. But our forces found certain signs by which they discovered the treason that those of Pazuco had planned against them. They attacked the place, and the enemy came out to meet them. They fought until they made them turn back and ousted them from the town, killing a great number of people.

73. On the conquest of Guatemala, see Lovell et al. (2013); on related Maya, Nahua, and Spanish primary sources, see Restall (1998), Restall and Asselbergs (2007), and Asselbergs (2008). On Nahua participation in the campaign, see Matthew (2012).

From here they went to Mopicalanco. They fought and did as they had done in other places. Then they went to a fortified place at the edge of the South Sea called Acaincatl. They found a great number of armed enemy warriors on a field at the entrance to this place. Our forces saw that the enemy held the advantage. There were at most 7,000 Mexica and Tezcuca, because the rest had either died or been disabled in battle and stayed in Quauhtemalan. Alvarado had no more than 250 Spaniards on foot and 100 horsemen and a few thousand from Quauhtemalan. Our forces decided to skirt around the enemy army, but they were seen and attacked. Our forces fought vigorously, and there were hardly any enemy survivors. They could not flee like others had, because they were wearing heavy armor that covered their full body, like sacks, and they carried lances that were longer than thirty hand spans. All of these people from the province of Caltipar were of Tolteca descent.

On this day many of our forces were wounded and others killed. Many Spaniards also were wounded, among them Alvarado, who was injured by an arrow that pierced his leg. Once this battle was over, our forces faced a fiercer one. A great army came well prepared with their long lances held high. Our forces toiled greatly and faced many risks in this struggle. Assailing the enemy, they quickly defeated them. From here they went to the province of Mahuatlan and defeated them. And from here they went to Athelechuan. Those from Cuitlachan met them there and offered their allegiance; our forces accompanied them to their town. They entered the city cautiously, because they had been warned that the inhabitants wanted to betray them and kill them. Our generals talked to them about surrendering, but they left and abandoned the city, leaving our forces alone. Each day they returned to wage war on our forces.

At the end of twenty days, seeing that those in this province would not surrender and could not be defeated by any means, our forces turned back to Quauhtemalan. I have not recorded all the details of this campaign, in which our forces suffered great hardship, hunger, and calamities, and the Spaniards found little gold and riches. However, many provinces were defeated and won. It is said that they traveled more than four hundred leagues, and the Aculhua and Mexica army came back from Quauhtemalan, leaving behind Alvarado and the rest of the Spaniards. When they reached Mexico, they told Ixtlilxochitl and King Quauhtemoc everything that had happened on their journey and gave some letters to Cortés, who was very pleased to hear all the good news. Cortés quickly sent Alvarado 200 Spaniards to settle in Quauhtemalan.

Two days after Alvarado left for Quauhtemalan, Cortés, Ixtlilxochitl, Quauhtemoc, and the other lords sent forces to Chamolan.[74] This was on December 8, 1523. Diego de Godoy went with 100 Spaniards on foot and 30 horsemen. Two generals, kinsmen of Ixtlilxochitl and Quauhtemoc, took 10,000 warriors each; one led the Aculhua, and the other led the Mexica and Tepaneca. They went straight to the Villa del Espíritu Santo, and there more Spaniards joined them. They undertook several expeditions, among them the one to Chamolan. It is a great province with a well-fortified city surrounded by a wall over eighteen feet high, made half of stone and half of wood, on top of a hill that is dangerous to climb. They fought for two days, during which the natives from the Aculhua and Mexica armies fought fiercely. The inhabitants who were besieged lacked food and took up their belongings and fled. Our forces entered the city and killed all those they found. They plundered the city and houses and supplied themselves with what little they found. Once this place was defeated they went to Chiapan and Huehueiztlan and were received peacefully.

On February 5, 1524, they sent another army against those of the Mixteca and Zapoteca, who had rebelled again and did great harm to their neighbors, who were allies of the Spaniards. And so Cortés sent Rodrigo Rangel, who had gone the first time, with 150 Spaniards. Ixtlilxochitl sent 20,000 warriors with them and one of his brothers as their general. On the way they joined with those from Tlaxcala, who numbered 5,000 or 6,000 men. When they arrived in those provinces, they demanded their surrender over and over again. Seeing that they would not surrender, they waged war and killed and captured many of them. As they had done previously, they sold the rest into slavery. Once they had defeated them, they returned to Mexico laden with plunder and the Spaniards with much gold, for it was a rich land. And thus the whole empire of the three capitals—Tezcuco, Mexico, and Tlacopan—was conquered. This region covered nearly four

---

74. This is a different expedition. It happened concurrently with Alvarado's expedition to Guatemala.

hundred leagues. It stretched from the big lake of Tezcuco all the way to the coasts of the South Sea and the North Sea, as we have seen.

Our forces undertook many more expeditions besides the ones mentioned here, but because nothing significant happened during any of them, they are not included to avoid verbosity. Ixtlilxochitl, his brothers, kinsmen, and vassals helped in all of them. It took great effort and huge expense to feed and house the Spaniards. It is widely known that, along with his vassals, Ixtlilxochitl personally helped the Christians as a service to God and our lord the emperor. He supported them and gave all of them as much gold, silver, and jewels as he could find in the palaces of his father and grandfather and even what his brothers and kinsmen had. This was in addition to the aforementioned amounts paid to ransom his two brothers, King Cacama and Cohuanacoch. Additionally, he spent a great portion of his assets to supply the armies that were sent to different places in the war for Mexico. He provided rations, prizes, and salaries to his soldiers, many of whom paid with their lives, as did many captains, lords, and nobles, who were his kinsmen.

Around the middle of the year 1524, which the natives call *chiquasen tecpatl*, 6 Flint, fray Martín de Valencia, the papal vicar, came to this land with twelve religious brothers of the Order of Saint Francis. They were the first to baptize and convert the natives to the law of the Gospel.[75] As soon as they heard that they had reached the port,[76] Ixtlilxochitl, Quauhtemoc, and the rest of the lords sent their messengers to welcome them and provide them with all that they needed for their journey to Mexico. When the messengers arrived, they welcomed them on behalf of their lords, attending to them along the way. Wherever they went, they were received with much celebration and rejoicing by the natives. Three leagues outside of Tezcuco, Cortés, Ixtlilxochitl, and the other lords and Spaniards, including fray Pedro de Gante, came out to greet them with joy and dancing. They

75. On the ambitious aims of the Franciscan mission to New Spain, see Phelan (1970). The order played a crucial role in the establishment of the colonial system and the transformation of indigenous society. On the other hand, the ethnohistoric and linguistic research conducted by Franciscan brethren, including such luminaries as Bernardino de Sahagún (1499–1590) and Alonso de Molina (ca. 1513–79), helped preserve much of what we know about pre-Hispanic Nahua culture and language.

76. Veracruz.

reached the city of Tezcuco, where they were hosted and entertained by the natives with great pleasure.

Father fray Pedro de Gante asked Ixtlilxochitl for furnishings and tapestries to decorate one of the rooms in their lodgings, which were the palaces of King Nezahualcoyotl. Ixtlilxochitl ordered the stewards who kept the tributes and treasure of Nezahualcoyotl to provide everything they requested. Father fray Pedro set up an altar, on which he placed an image of Our Lady and a small crucifix. On this day, which was the eve of the feast day of Saint Anthony of Padua,[77] vespers[78] were celebrated very solemnly. They were the first to be celebrated in this land. The next day they celebrated a sung Mass with great solemnity. It was the first Mass that these religious[79] celebrated in New Spain.

Cortés and all the Spaniards and Ixtlilxochitl with all the lords, his brothers, and kinsmen heard the Mass attentively. They were so moved by joy that they cried at seeing what they had so desired, especially because they were very aware of the meaning of the Mass. Father fray Pedro de Gante, as best he could, and truly by the grace of God, had instructed them in Christian doctrine and the mysteries of the life and passion of Jesus Christ while he walked the earth, as well as in the law of the Gospel. So when they heard this first Mass, they knew well what it was about. And Ixtlilxochitl was so moved that he began weeping, and this inspired awe and devotion in the friars and Spaniards who were there.

Father Gante informed Father fray Martín de Valencia that Ixtlilxochitl and the rest of his lords, kinsmen, and vassals wanted to be baptized. Thus Father Gante began baptizing in the city of Tezcuco, which was the first place where the law of the Gospel was established. The first to be baptized was Ixtlilxochitl, who took the name don Fernando, after the Catholic king.[80] Father fray Martín de Valencia baptized him himself, and his godfather was Cortés. Then his brother Cohuanacoch took the name don Pedro; they say that his godfather was Alvarado, who was in Tezcuco at the time. Then don Pedro Tetlahuehuezquititzin, don Juan Quauhtliztactzin, and don Jorge

---

77. June 12.

78. The evening prayer service.

79. A religious is a member of the Catholic regular clergy, so called because they follow a *regula*, or rule, associated with a specific order, for example, the Franciscans.

80. Ferdinand II of Aragon (r. 1479–1516), known as "the Catholic."

Yoyontzin, his legitimate brothers, were baptized. And then the rest of his brothers, his father's illegitimate sons, don Carlos Ahuaxpitzactzin, don Antonio Tlahuitoltzin, don Francisco Moxiuhquecholtzomatzin, and don Lorenzo de Luna were baptized. The rest of his uncles, cousins, and kinsmen were baptized.

Since she was Mexica and somewhat hardened in her idolatry, Ixtlilxochitl's mother, Queen Tlacoxhuatzin, refused to be baptized and went to a temple in the city with a few lords. Ixtlilxochitl went there and begged her to be baptized. She scolded him and spoke harshly, telling him that she did not want to get baptized and that he was crazy for being so quick to disown his gods and the faith of his ancestors. Seeing his mother's stubbornness, Ixtlilxochitl got very angry and threatened to burn her alive if she would not be baptized. He finally convinced her with many arguments and brought her to the church with the other lords so that they could be baptized. Then he burned down the temple where she had been. This queen was the first woman to be baptized, and she took the name doña María. Her godfather was Cortés. After her, Papantzin, the woman who had been the wife of Cuitlahua and who was now Ixtlilxochitl's legitimate wife, was baptized and took the name doña Beatriz, out of consideration for Cortés. Cortés was her godfather, because Ixtlilxochitl was his friend and loyal ally.

After these baptisms, the rest of the nobles and then the city's commoners were baptized. The religious spent several days baptizing the people. Meanwhile, Ixtlilxochitl taught his brothers, kinsmen, and relatives about the Christian doctrine, along with Castilian customs, ceremonies, and manners, which were very different from those of this land. He gave long speeches and sermons recalling great things. He moved them with his good and saintly words as if he were an apostle, so to speak. Many of them were set in their ancient ways, so, in spite of Ixtlilxochitl's teaching, they were not able to learn the Castilian way of showing respect and other social graces. For example, a lady who was Ixtlilxochitl's sister went to visit Father fray Martín de Valencia and wanted to curtsy in the Castilian way as her brother had commanded. But she genuflected, as a man would, and the religious laughed heartily. Being a noble lady, she asked with great courtesy for them to forgive her if she had done something inappropriate. She said she had not understood the teachings of her brother, and since she had seen some gentlemen greet them in that way, just as Cortés and his men did, she thought that it was the way both men and women showed respect. In this land both men and women greet in the same way, by bowing the head. There were many other improprieties in the early days. They were committed as much by the natives as by the Spaniards, and they caused great laughter on both sides. But in the end, even though these manners were new and had never been seen, heard, or done, they were easily learned in a short time.

By this time all the houses in Mexico had been finished except for a few that belonged to the Spaniards, which were still being built. Ixtlilxochitl was readying his soldiers and everything they would need for the upcoming journey to Yhueras.[81] Cortés sent to the emperor in Spain a large amount of gold, precious feathers, blankets, and other jewels, including a cannon made of silver. Ixtlilxochitl and the other lords did the same, asking Cortés to write to the emperor on their behalf, offering their services, kingdoms, and vassals to do his will. Cortés said he would do so and that His Majesty was well informed and very thankful for their contributions that Cortés had accepted on the emperor's behalf. He was even more pleased that they were being baptized and welcoming the law of the Gospel, which was what His Majesty desired most. Whether Cortés actually wrote on their behalf—especially on behalf of Ixtlilxochitl, whose role in establishing the law of the Gospel is second only to God's, as we have seen and is well known—is known only to him. But Ixtlilxochitl did not receive any reply, and if His Majesty sent him any messages, it was not through Cortés but through the Franciscan friars. After Ixtlilxochitl's death, his very young heirs, especially doña Ana and doña Luisa, who were his legitimate daughters, had no one on their side. He was buried and forgotten, and his descendants were left poor and neglected. They hardly have houses to live in, and every day these are taken away.

In that same year, a few days before the journey to Yhueras, the city of Tezcuco served as the venue for a synod,[82] which was the

---

81. Also Higueras or Hibueras. The region beyond Guatemala, roughly corresponding to modern-day Honduras. The expedition's goal was to prevent Cristóbal de Olid from establishing an autonomous colony in defiance of Cortés's authority. Cortés related the journey to Hibueras in his fifth letter to Charles V.

82. An assembly of the clergy (and sometimes also of some of the laity) of an ecclesiastical jurisdiction.

first to be held in this New Spain. They addressed marriage and other issues. There were thirty scholars, five clerics, nineteen friars, and six lay lawyers, including Cortés. It was presided over by fray Martín de Valencia as papal vicar. Since the marriage rituals were not well understood, it was decided that at that time they could marry whomever they wanted. After the synod the friars and the clerics fanned out across the land, especially in the big cities such as Mexico, Tlacopan, Xochimilco, Tlaxcala, Cholula, and the rest.

In Tezcuco they began building the first church in this New Spain. It was named after Saint Anthony of Padua because the first Mass was said on his feast day. Saint Anthony is the patron of the city, and the church is built where Nezahualcoyotl's palaces used to be, even though now they are in ruins, and streets run through them. The city of Tezcuco and the houses of Nezahualcoyotl have been very fortunate, especially in heavenly matters. Nezahualcoyotl did not have the good fortune to see so much good, since it was not yet God's will, but he desired it and foresaw it. And so for this reason these houses should be greatly esteemed, since it was where the law of the Gospel was first established. It was also where the mysteries of Christ's life and passion for the redemption of humankind, especially these barbarians, were first performed. Moreover, it was the first place where the host of his most holy body and blood was consecrated. Nezahualcoyotl's heirs, who are poor and whose dominions and patrimony have been taken away, have not been able to maintain the palaces. Some Spaniards have usurped them: the place where the first Mass was said by those blessed first religious is now used by the Spaniards as a workshop.

Once it was time to go to Yhueras, which was around the month of October, Ixtlilxochitl decided to review the number of soldiers in his army in the square of Otumpan, where he lived. He chose twenty thousand warriors who were the bravest and whom he knew from the previous campaigns, along with all the captains who were friends and servants who had always followed him. He appointed Alonso Yzquinquani, his servant, in his stead as the lieutenant governor of the whole kingdom of Tezcuco, even though half of it belonged to his brother Cohuanacoch. But Ixtlilxochitl was in charge of all of it because Cohuanacoch only received tribute and recognition. In all things concerning government, especially war matters, he did not meddle. Cortés had decided this because he was afraid Cohuanacoch

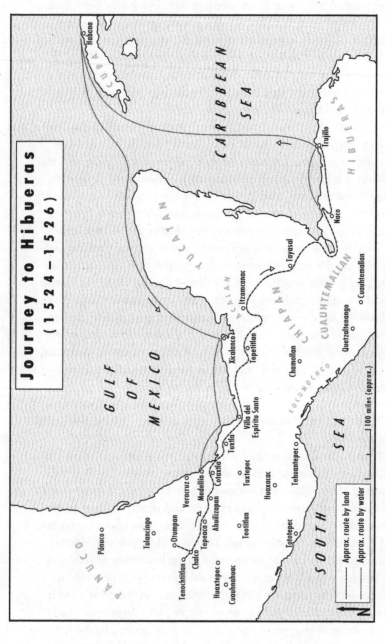

Cortés's punitive expedition against Cristóbal de Olid was costly, arduous, and ultimately fruitless. Map by Pablo García.

might rebel. Ixtlilxochitl decided not to leave the government in the hands of any of his brothers and kinsmen for many important reasons. For one, they were very young, and it would not be in keeping with their status to be subject to or attend to the Spaniards. Additionally, he did not want his brothers to falsely accuse Ixtlilxochitl of wanting to rebel against the Spaniards, as Nonohualcatzin did in the time of his brother King Cacama.

This Alonso Yzquinquani, his servant, was a smart and generous man and very capable. He also left another two governors called Zontecon and Cohuatecatl for the two other capitals, Mexico and Tlacopan. They would be subject to Yzquinquani. Ixtlilxochitl made the arrangements and put the governors in place for the kingdom of the Aculhua and for the Mexica and Tepaneca since he was in charge of everything, as we have seen; King Quauhtemoc and King Tetlepanquetzal were imprisoned and did not participate in matters related to the governing of their kingdoms. Ixtlilxochitl left Otumpan and traveled to Chalco, where he waited for Cortés, who, having appointed his lieutenants in Mexico City,[83] left with as many Spaniards as he could gather. He was well supplied with weapons and all the necessities. As further insurance against rebellion, he took with him King Quauhtemoc, Cohuanacoch, Tetlepanquetzal, and Zihuancohuatl, who was the governor and captain general of the Mexica,[84] as well as Tlacatecatzin and Mexitzincotzin, who were the most powerful and noble lords of the land. When they reached Chalco, Cortés joined Ixtlilxochitl, and the two of them marched with the whole army with great haste, because Cortés was distraught by the news that Cristóbal de Olid had rebelled against him.[85] He wanted to quell the insurrection before the situation escalated. On the way he also wanted to subdue certain provinces that were in rebellion because the Spaniards had stolen their belongings and mistreated them a thousand times over.

83. The appointees were the *tesorero* (treasurer) Alonso de Estrada, the *contador* (accountant) Rodrigo de Albornoz, and Alonso Zuazo. Estrada and Albornoz were soon at odds with each other and their government in crisis (Gómara 1979, 320).

84. Zihuancohuatl is a corruption of *Cihuacoatl*, which is not a name but the title of the Mexica ruler's senior adviser (Aguilar-Moreno 2006, 86).

85. Unbeknownst to Cortés, Olid was already dead. Francisco de las Casas, who had earlier been sent to subdue Olid, was on his way back to Mexico to report on the success of his mission when Cortés set out to deal personally with the rebellious officer (Martínez 1987, 114).

A few days after Cortés had left Mexico, the Spanish governors that he left in his stead, Alonso de Estrada and Rodrigo de Albornoz, had certain disputes and disagreements over governance, so all the Spaniards were fighting against one another. The natives suffered greatly; they would have risen up and killed all the Spaniards in the city had it not been for the love of the religious, who calmed them down. The friars also asked the Spaniards not to mistreat the natives so badly, so they would not rise up in rebellion, since they easily could have done so. Moreover, everyone was sad and complained, saying that their lord kings were taken by Cortés, almost like prisoners, to faraway lands. They thought that he was taking them to kill them treacherously and secretively, as in fact happened.

The Spaniards were very angry with the friars because they took the Indians' side, and so they very nearly threw them out of Mexico. There was even one time, when a certain religious was preaching and castigating the Spaniards for their evil deeds and tyrannies, the Spaniards rose against this friar and almost threw him down from the pulpit. But owing to the saintly wisdom and prudence of fray Martín de Valencia, the friars, with the love of God in their hearts, tolerated from the Spaniards what they would have expected of the barbarous Indians. The messengers that came and went each day told Ixtlilxochitl and the other kings and lords everything. Ixtlilxochitl sent word to Yzquinquani, his governor, that if the friars were harassed by the Spaniards they should go to the city of Tezcuco. He should give them everything they needed and guard them day and night to keep the Spaniards from bothering them. When Alonso Yzquinquani heard this message, he followed his lord's instructions precisely. The friars who could not suffer the Spaniards' misdeeds went to Tezcuco, where, along with the friars who were already there, they were welcomed and well treated by the natives. They say that there were as many as nine of them, and they were in Tezcuco until Cortés and Ixtlilxochitl returned.

From the Villa del Espíritu Santo, Cortés sent the *factor*,[86] Gonzalo de Salazar, and the *veedor*,[87] Peralmides Chirino de Úbeda, as his lieutenants to govern. They were to relieve Alonso de Estrada and

---

86. Commercial agent. One of the four royal officials, along with the *tesorero*, the *contador*, and the *veedor*, in charge of collecting royal income. The *factor* was specifically in charge of in-kind income.

87. Inspector. The royal official in charge of income paid in coin or precious metals.

Rodrigo de Albornoz of their duties and punish them if they were to blame for the revolt. When they arrived in Mexico, instead of appeasing and disciplining the Spaniards, their arrival inspired much hatred and further revolt among the king's officials. A civil war erupted.[88] Many Spaniards died, and Mexico was nearly lost. If it seemed that they had mistreated the natives before, it was much worse during these revolts, in which they did them a thousand wrongs and stole their properties.

The natives in Huaxacac, Zihuatlan, and other places, who also suffered the abuses of the Spaniards in their lands—especially certain miners who kidnapped Indians for their mines—were in rebellion. Peralmides attacked them with one hundred Spaniards on horseback and two hundred on foot, backed by I do not know how many thousands of Aculhua and Mexica natives that Ixtlilxochitl's governor had provided. As they got there, they waged war. The natives escaped to the rocky hills. Even though Peralmides saw that the enemy was very strong and could not be defeated, he persisted in his campaign because he found out that they had much gold and riches, including a big golden snake. He besieged them for forty days, at the end of which the natives absconded with all the treasure one night without being heard and fooled the Spaniards. They tried to catch up to them in Cihuatlan, but they were never able to defeat them. And with this they returned to Mexico, where great things happened that I do not include since they are not a part of my history. Let whoever wants to know the details read *La crónica de las Indias*.[89] There they will find a very complete account of everything concerning the Spaniards. My sole intention is to tell the story of the lords of this land, especially don Fernando Ixtlilxochitl and his brothers and kinsmen, whose heroic deeds are all but forgotten. No one remembers them or the help they provided the Spaniards, as we have seen and as we will see in what follows.

---

88. Salazar and Peralmíndez (Pedro Almíndez) ousted Estrada, Albornoz, and Zuazo. Soon after, Salazar appointed himself governor, announcing that Cortés was dead. When Martín Dorantes brought proof to the contrary, Cortés's supporters rallied behind Estrada and Albornoz to bring down Salazar, who was imprisoned along with Almíndez. Later Estrada, Salazar, and Almíndez joined forces against Cortés (Gómara 1979, 322–24, 362). On the Byzantine details of these quarrels, see Porras Muñoz (1978).

89. Gómara's *Historia de la conquista de México*, first published in 1552.

During the period that Alonso de Estrada was governor, he meted out punishments, chastened the Spaniards, and brought peace to Mexico. This clearly shows that Quauhtemoc and the rest of the lords died unjustly and that they were falsely accused; their vassals never rose up or took up arms against the Spaniards. Even though the vassals complained about the wrongs the Spaniards committed against them, their lords always replied that they should bear it with the love of God. They also said to follow the example of their kings and lords and consider their long and arduous journey, which was filled with hardships, and on which they were famished, sunburned, and frostbitten. Since their lords bore it with much patience, they should do the same. And so it is true, as I have said, that the hopeless and persecuted natives would not have left a single Spaniard alive if it had not been for the love of their lords. They could have killed them all easily because, unlike Cortés, these Spaniards had no support in Tezcuco, Tlaxcala, and other lands and provinces, and they were fighting against one another. But those who have written or said that Quauhtemoc and the others were killed because they wanted to kill the Spaniards, say this only, as is well known, to cover up their misdeeds and treason. Perhaps we could believe them if there were a native history or native person who said this to be true, but there is no history or account that does. All the histories, accounts, and natives of New Spain agree that it was a false accusation and an act of great tyranny. I say this in response to what the Spanish historians have written, and I am not surprised, since they have written based on the accounts provided by Cortés and the others who were so cruel. Those who have written afterward have followed these sources without further clarifying or finding out the truth.

Once Cortés and the others, who were on their way to Yhueras, arrived at the Villa del Espíritu Santo, Ixtlilxochitl and Quauhtemoc sent word to the lords of Tabaxco and Chicalanco, saying that they had arrived and that they were on their way to Yhueras with Cortés. They requested a painting showing all the roads, towns, and places that they would find along the way and the rivers they would have to cross. They also asked to be sent merchants who knew the land and coasts and could guide them. After hearing what the kings had ordered, the lords of Tabaxco and Xicalanco had the entire route and the landmarks they would pass quickly painted. Once the painting was done, they sent it with around ten very knowledgeable nobles, so they could explain the painting. When they presented themselves on behalf of their lords, they showed the painting that they had been ordered to make, which showed the route from Xicalanco to Naco and Nito and all the way to Nicarahua.[90] Once Ixtlilxochitl and the rest of the lords had seen the painting, they showed it to Cortés, who was greatly pleased and thanked those from Tabaxco and Xicalanco.

Cortés was also told that most of the places they would go through were uninhabited, because the Spaniards had robbed and burned them, and the natives had fled to the deserts. And so they left the Villa del Espíritu Santo after having sent supply ships down the Tabaxco River. They had traveled eight or nine leagues when they crossed a very wide river on barges, and they reached Tonalan. They walked the same number of leagues to another river called Qui-yahuilco. From there it was a short trek to another very big river near the sea. In order to cross it, it was necessary to build a wooden bridge that was almost one thousand yards across. The natives worked hard because it was they who built this bridge. Then they walked for another thirty or forty leagues, crossing fifty rivers, where the natives were put to work building many bridges until they reached the province of Copilco and the town of Anaxaxucan, the last in this province.

They left and walked across very rough mountains, and they crossed a large river called Quetzalapan. Since this river ran into the Tabaxco, they were able to get food from the ships in some of the canoes that many natives had brought. They also used them to take the army across. They spent twenty days in Zihuatlan. From here they went to Chilapan, where they built another bridge to cross another river. Chilapan had been burned and destroyed by the Spaniards, like the other places. And so it was abandoned and without inhabitants, except for two men who were waiting for them. They knew from the guides that the Spaniards, their kings, and the whole army were coming; this province was subject to the city of Tezcuco. They crossed a big river called Chilapan, and, guided by these two men, they went to Tamaztepec. It took them two days to cross four or five leagues, which was the most they could do. It took that long because the road was difficult and flooded, and it was challenging for our forces. At Tamaztepec they spent six days resting and resupplied their food stores, because they found much maize and many fruits.

90. Nicaragua.

From here it took them two days to travel to Iztapan, which took as much effort as the previous leg. Seeing the Spaniards, the people of Iztapan fled with their women and children, each carrying as much of their belongings as they could because they were scared. They had heard about all the evil deeds they had done to the neighboring towns, which the people of Zihuatlan had told them about. Many of them drowned trying to cross the river. Ixtlilxochitl sent word for them to return, saying he would do them no harm. When they heard and realized that their kings were in fact there, they returned with their lord, welcomed them, and provided everything they needed during the eight days the army was there. From here Cortés sent some canoes downriver to Tabaxco with three Spaniards with instructions to wait for him in the Bay of Ascensión.[91] The plan was to take supplies from the ship to Acalan[92] by way of an estuary. Cortés also sent canoes with a number of people and some Spaniards upriver to pacify some towns that were in rebellion.

After all this, they left Iztapan for Tlatlahuitlapan. When they arrived, they found the town abandoned but for twenty native priests in a temple on the bank of the river. Our forces crossed a swamp with great difficulty and came to a deep marsh, across which they built a bridge. Then they went through another swamp that was more than a league across and then reached a heavily wooded mountain with trees so tall they could hardly see the sky. They were lost on this mountain for two days. On the third day they ended up in Ahuatecpan, where they satisfied their hunger with fruits. This place was also abandoned. Cortés and Ixtlilxochitl sent some canoes upriver to determine if the Spaniards and the other people who were sailing on the river had gone by. Walking through fields, they discovered a lake, where they saw a lot of townspeople on some small islands and in canoes. Seeing our forces, these people came to them, laughing along the way, because they had never seen bearded Spaniards dressed as they were. Ixtlilxochitl's men explained the situation to them, and understanding that they were not going to be harmed, they loaded food, honey, and other gifts into their

91. In the modern Mexican state of Quintana Roo.
92. In the modern Mexican state of Campeche. On the region, the Chontal people, and the conquest of Acalan, see Scholes and Roys (1968). On the Chontal account of the first contact with the Spaniards, see Restall (1998).

canoes. They went to see the kings and Cortés. They apologized and said that they had left their town because they had heard in Zihuatlan that some Spaniards had robbed and burned many towns. They also told them that the Spaniards whom they were looking for were in a town upriver. A brother of their lord and some warriors had gone with them to ensure that the natives upriver would not hurt them. Cortés sent for the Spaniards upriver, and they returned loaded with much honey, cacao beans, food, and some gold. All the natives returned to their houses. All the neighboring towns and places came to see the kings and Cortés to offer their alliance. Each one gave what little gold they had to Cortés, because Quauhtemoc had ordered them to do so.

They left this town of Ahuatecpan after having burned the idols and temples and set up crosses. Two friars instructed them in the law of the Gospel through their interpreters, who accompanied them. Ixtlilxochitl and the other lords also preached to them, bringing great things to mind. They took a path that goes straight to the province of Acalan. They crossed a big river on some barges and walked for three days across very rough mountains, where they suffered much hardship. Ixtlilxochitl, Quauhtemoc, and the rest of their vassals were very tired from hunger and thirst, because they ate nothing but plants. Although they had some maize, the Spaniards preferred to give it to their horses than to the army. At the end of three days, they came to an estuary that was more than five hundred feet wide and about six fathoms deep. Since they had no canoes to cross to the other side, they worked hard to build a huge bridge, at great risk to the natives because of the depth. Building it took six full days and caused the natives great misery and hunger; even their kings and lords suffered, eating nothing but plants and wild berries, and these were so hard to find that they could barely get a mouthful. The vassals did their lords a great kindness by giving them some maize kernels that they stole from the horses. The Spaniards cared more for the beasts than for the kings and great lords. They had taken the horses to impress the natives of those lands, who had never seen them, because rumors about them had spread through the land. The horses, however, were not necessary to fight in this land, because it was very rough, and all the flat areas were swamps or lakes. It was a miracle that they rode them at all; the road was so difficult that mostly they were forced to walk on foot.

It would take a whole book just to write the account of the hardships suffered by Ixtlilxochitl, Quauhtemoc, Cohuanacoch, and the other lords and their vassals in just the time it took to build this bridge, in addition to all that has been said before and shall be said. This demonstrates that the accusations against Quauhtemoc and the rest of the lords were lies. They were too burdened with work and suffered misery and hunger; they saw that the Spaniards did not even want them to eat, but would willingly kill them all if they could. These people never complained or showed weakness; rather, they gladly did what they were ordered to do. If they had wanted to kill the Spaniards, they could have done so easily without any risk. Or else they could have left in the night, leaving the Spaniards lost, and returned to Mexico. It was easier for them than the Spaniards, for they had guides and would be better welcomed wherever they went than they would have been with the Spaniards, because the people in the region were their vassals. They could, as they say, incite their kingdoms and vassals against the Spaniards. But instead, even though they were barbarians, they well knew that the Spaniards brought the true light, the law of the Gospel, and the salvation of their souls, which they longed for. And so they loved them greatly. They suffered hunger and hardship so that the Spaniards and the beasts in their service would not have to; they took the food from their mouths to feed them.

This bridge was the most impressive thing in the world, and the Spaniards were awed to see the skill and the ability with which the natives built it. Once it was finished, they crossed it, and after a short time they came to a frightening swamp, but it was not very wide. The horses were not able to cross, so they decided to cut a ditch through the middle of it, through which the horses were able to swim. Once they were on the other side, more than one hundred natives came to greet them, bearing food and refreshment. Along with them were four Spaniards and some soldiers who had gone with them to let the king of the province of Acalan know of their arrival. The king was called Apoxpalon. This lord was very happy knowing that his kings and great lords were coming to visit him in his land, where he was waiting to receive them and the Spaniards. With these people he sent gifts for Cortés, Ixtlilxochitl, Cohuanacoch, and the other lords, giving each one his share and welcoming them. He also sent word that he had been waiting for them for many days, because the people in

Xicalanco had informed him that they were coming to his lands and given him other news. A similar message was sent to Cortés. Everyone was greatly pleased by the care and good will that Apoxpalon had for them, and so the messengers returned.

The next day they left this place and went to Tizapetlac, where they were received with many celebrations. They were welcomed and provided with food and everything they needed. They rested here for four or five days, after which they left for Teotlicac, two days' journey beyond Acalan. They arrived early in the morning on the bank of the big river, the same one that lets out at Cohuatzacualco. When they arrived, they built some huts or lodgings made of straw so that Cortés and his men could stay in them. They built separate ones for their kings behind the main temple. The Spaniards were celebrating Carnival,[93] just as the natives had seen them do in years past, which coincided with native celebrations. Following their ancient custom, the natives greatly rejoiced this day and night. It was common for our forces to celebrate when they reached a new place, but here the rejoicing was greater for the aforementioned reasons, and because they were nearing the end of this long journey. Cortés had told them that from Acalan they would turn back without going any farther. They all were happy. The kings were having a lighthearted conversation with one another.

Cohuanacoch joked with King Quauhtemoc, "My lord, the province we are going to conquer will be mine, because, as Your Highness knows, the city of Tezcuco and my kingdoms are always given preference in all things, according to the laws of my grandfather Nezahualcoyotl and the agreements he made with his uncle Izcohuatl,[94] Your Highness's ancestor." Laughing, King Quauhtemoc replied, "In those times, my lord, our armies went alone, and it was right that Your Majesty have priority, since the city of Tezcuco is our ancient homeland and where our lineage comes from. But now the children of the sun are helping us, and because they love me so much, the province will be for my royal crown." Tetlepanquetzal jumped up and said, "No my lord. Since the world is upside down, let it all be for me. Tlacopan and the kingdom of the Tepaneca was the last to receive its portion; let it now be the first."

93. In the Catholic Church calendar, the days just before the beginning of Lent.
94. Itzcoatl (r. 1427–40), fourth tlatoani of Mexico-Tenochtitlan.

Temilotzin, who was a general of the kingdom of Mexico and one
of the greatest lords and who had the title of Tlacatecatl, sighed and
said, "Oh, my lords! How Your Highnesses jest about the chicken
taken by the greedy wolf that no hunter can take from him, or the
little chick snatched by the crafty hawk when its caretaker is away,
no matter how much the mother defends him. My lord King Quauhtemoc defended his homeland like a good father, but the Chichimeca
Empire lacked the peace and harmony that safeguards a kingdom.
Our arrogance and discord delivered us into the hands of these foreigners to suffer these long and harsh journeys, hunger, the cold, and
a thousand other calamities. Our kingdoms and dominions have been
taken away, and we ourselves have been forgotten by our generous
homeland as if we were its enemies. But it was all worth it, since our
friends, the children of the sun, have brought us the true light, the
salvation of our souls and the life everlasting, from which we were
so far removed as we enjoyed the worldly delights and the horrible
darkness, doing what our false gods ordered us to do, sacrificing our
fellow men. We thought that we were right in our ancient customs, but we were bound for the abyss of hell. Oh, Nezahualcoyotl
and Nezahualpilli, wisest of kings, what joy it would have brought
you to see this blessed time you so longed for! Oh, you who spoke
against our errors many times! So much more fortunate are we,
who enjoy these times and our worthwhile labors that will bring two
rewards: one in this life, which is honor and fame without regard
for the fleeting riches of this world; and the other, in the everlasting
life with Tloque Nahuaque,[95] whom the Castilians call Jesus Christ.
And so, my lords, let Your Highnesses be consoled, and bear these
labors patiently. Heed the example of these children of the sun, who
traverse such great seas and endure such long journeys and hardships
for the well-being of our souls. Let us do as Ixtlilxochitl. Your Highnesses will never see any trace of sorrow on his face. He is the most
diligent in his labor and, for the sake of the Gospel, has forsaken his
homeland, kinsmen, and friends. Listen carefully to the Christian
priests, and you will see how my words are true, when the friars
preach to us." This lord continued to speak and moved everyone with

95. According to Lockhart, "Tloque Nahuaque" means "possessor or master of
that which is near, close, in reference to God or in preconquest times to powerful indigenous deities" (2001, 239).

his words. They thanked him for his good advice. There were around nine lords at this gathering. They also spoke, relaxed, rejoiced, and sang the poems composed by the ancient philosophers, who foresaw everything that they were seeing and suffering.[96]

Seeing the lords bantering and joking, Cortés misinterpreted their merriment. As the proverb says, a thief believes that everyone steals. Cortés told them through interpreters[97] that it was not proper for lords and great princes to banter with one another, and he hoped that they would not do it again. They responded that it was not their intent to upset him but rather to get some respite from their hardships; on occasions such as these it is good for princes to appear as happy as if they were in their courts and palaces so that their vassals will have the courage and strength to endure their hardships. They agreed with him that it was highly inappropriate to show such merriment when they were not at war or in other times of crisis. And since Cortés did not approve, for his sake they would not banter any more with one another.

Later Cortés secretly summoned an Indian named Coztemexi, who was later called Cristóbal. He was a native of Iztapalapan or, according to others, Mexicalcinco. Cortés had great trust in him, for he always told Cortés everything that was said or done by those in the army. There are always troublemakers in the world and wicked tongues that cut more deeply than sharp knives. Cortés asked Cristóbal what the lords' long speeches were about. In agreement with popular opinion, and according to Cristóbal's later confession, which was made when Ixtlilxochitl tortured him to figure out what he told Cortés that could have led to the unjust deaths of so many kings and lords,[98] he said that he told Cortés what had happened, as it was described earlier. And Cortés ordered Cristóbal to paint and document who was at the gathering. And he painted nine people. But Cristóbal maintained that he did not say what Cortés said he said, namely, that the kings wanted to rise up and kill all the Spaniards. All the histories,

96. This fictional scene neatly encapsulates the defining traits of Alva Ixtlilxochitl's historiography: Tetzcoco's primacy as the capital of the ancient Chichimeca Empire, Nezahualcoyotl's monotheistic intuition, Ixtlilxochitl's exemplary devotion to the Christian cause, and prophecy as the drive of history.

97. In the manuscript "Marina" is crossed out and "las interpretes" is inserted (CC INAH, vol. 2, fol. 58r).

98. The deaths of the kings and lords are described in the following paragraph.

paintings, and other accounts confirm the confession of this Indian, whom Cortés presented as a witness and caused the blameless lords to die. But, in truth, Cortés made up all these things to unburden himself and so that no natural lord of the land would remain.

The next day, Shrove Tuesday[99] of the year 1525, three hours before dawn, Cortés called the kings and lords one by one, without the others' knowledge so that they would not get agitated and threaten him and his men. He hanged them one by one: first King Quauhtemoc, then Tetlepanquetzal, and the rest (fig. 3).[100] Last of all was Cohuanacoch. But Ixtlilxochitl, who was informed that the kings had been hanged and that his brother was being hanged, quickly left his lodgings and started raising the alarm and rousing his army against Cortés and his men. Seeing the dire straits that he and his men were in, and with no other solution, Cortés ran up to the gallows and cut the rope that was around the neck of Cohuanacoch, who was now gasping for air. Cortés begged Ixtlilxochitl to listen to him, saying that he wanted to explain why he had done this. If afterward he did not think it was fair, then he could do whatever he wanted. Ixtlilxochitl ordered the army to stand down, because they were ready to tear the Spaniards to pieces. Ixtlilxochitl listened attentively to Cortés, who gave him the account painted by Coztemexi and told him that Quauhtemoc and Cohuanacoch and the other lords wanted to kill him and the rest of the Spaniards. With many other explanations, Cortés said that the most blameworthy was Ixtlilxochitl's brother Cohuanacoch and that he purposefully had not hanged him earlier, hoping that Ixtlilxochitl would wake up so that he could sentence him himself. But seeing that he was sleeping so peacefully, and in order not to bother him and excite all the people, he ordered him to be hanged. He said this and many other things. Having heard all the explanations, though with great sadness, Ixtlilxochitl calmed down. He remembered, among other things, his newfound faith and thought that if he took violent action at that moment, everything would be lost, the Gospel would not spread, and many wars would

99. The day before Ash Wednesday, the beginning of Lent.
100. In the Chontal account, Cuauhtemoc is (also?) decapitated (Restall 1998, 64). In the painted *Tira de Tepechpan*, Cuauhtemoc appears hanging by the feet with his head at an awkward angle. Restall (2003b) reviews the various versions of "Cuauhtemoc's betrayal."

FIG. 3 Codex Vaticanus (Vat. lat. 3738), folio 89r, detail. Cuauhtemoc's execution. The *tlatoani* is identified by his name glyph, "Descending Eagle." The event appears under the year sign 6 Flint (1524), coinciding with the arrival of the Franciscan missionaries to Mexico-Tenochtitlan, also represented. Photo reproduced by permission of and copyright 2015 by Biblioteca Apostolica Vaticana, with all rights reserved.

ensue. Believing it to be for the best, he decided to overlook this betrayal as best he could.

Once the day had dawned and peace between Cortés and Ixtlilxochitl was restored, they returned to Itzamcamac. Ixtlilxochitl ordered his men to carry his brother on a pallet, because his throat was injured from the rope with which they had meant to hang him. A few days later Cohuanacoch died from bloody diarrhea brought on by heartache and sadness. They were a day from Itzamcamac when the young son of Apoxpalon, the lord of Itzamcamac, came to meet them. He offered his condolences to Ixtlilxochitl on the death of the kings and lords; this news had reached all the towns of Acalan. He said his father was dead. (Apoxpalon had ordered his son to say that, because he did not want to see the Spaniards on account of the things they had done.) Ixtlilxochitl consoled Apoxpalon's son and ordered him to speak with Cortés, who was very happy to see him and gave him some things from Spain. However, Cortés would not believe that his father was dead, because it had only been a few days since his messengers had been sent, as has been said before.

They came to a town named Teotlycacac,[101] where they were welcomed and entertained. Cortés forged a strong friendship with the local lord, and he secretly asked him if it was true that Apoxpalon was dead. He answered confidentially that, in fact, he was not dead but was only pretending to be dead so that Cortés would not go into his lands; the whole region disapproved of the way he had killed the kings. Cortés explained why he had done it and gave him many other explanations that are not part of my story. Cortés then secretly called the son of Apoxpalon and told him that he knew for a fact that his father was alive. Seeing that he could no longer deny the truth, the young man told Cortés that his father was alive and the reasons for his refusal to meet him. Cortés asked him to send for him, and he also asked Ixtlilxochitl to send for him as well. Ixtlilxochitl sent some of his soldiers with the son of Apoxpalon to ask him to come immediately to meet him and Cortés. Apoxpalon came two days later and went first to Ixtlilxochitl's lodgings in some big temples, of which there were many in this town. Apoxpalon offered his condolences to Ixtlilxochitl and wept with him.[102] He then excused himself by saying that, because of the Spaniards' cruel deeds, he had told his son to tell the Spaniards he was dead to avoid meeting them. He asked Ixtlilxochitl to forgive him. Ixtlilxochitl thanked him for his words and escorted him to Cortés's lodgings, as he had requested. Apoxpalon told Cortés why he had refused to meet them and offer his alliance.

101. In fact, the expedition has not moved. According to the Chontal account, Pax-Bolon-Acha met Cortés in Tuxakha, the same place where Cuauhtemoc was executed (Restall 1998, 63–64). Tuxakha is called Teutiacar by Cortés (1986, 363), Teuticaccac by Gómara (1979, 332), and both Teotlicac and Teotlycacac by Alva Ixtlilxochitl, who apparently lost the narrative thread in the detailed description of the events surrounding the Nahua rulers' deaths.

102. In other versions Pax-Bolon-Acha comes to meet Cortés prior to Cuauhtemoc's execution. In the Chontal account the Mexica leader invites his Chontal counterpart to join in a rebellion against the Spaniards; Pax-Bolon-Acha refuses, revealing the conspiracy to Cortés instead (Restall 1998, 64). This should not, however, be taken as proof positive that the plot existed.

He asked Cortés and Ixtlilxochitl to go with him to Itzamcamac, his capital city, where they would be welcomed, attended to, and entertained.

The next day they left for Itzamcamac, and when they arrived there was much rejoicing and celebrating. They stayed in Apoxpalon's houses. Before entering the city, Ixtlilxochitl commanded Apoxpalon to order his architects to carve his likeness on a tall cliff that is near the road to Itzamcamac. Apoxpalon did as Ixtlilxochitl commanded. They carved his life-size likeness on the cliff. He was shown wearing the armor and weapons that he had on that occasion. It is said that it can still be seen today and is mentioned in the songs. Ixtlilxochitl did this so that his descendants would see his image there, and he would be remembered forever. As I say, the architects made such a faithful representation that not one thing was missing. Ixtlilxochitl went to see it with Apoxpalon, and there he was moved and wept, according to the songs. Apoxpalon and the other lords also wept, even as they consoled him. They spent a few days in Itzamcamac being well attended and entertained. Cortés and Ixtlilxochitl received many finely crafted gifts from Apoxpalon: *jícaras* and *tecomates* in different styles,[103] and many other things that can be found in this province, where all the natives are merchants. Ixtlilxochitl appreciated these gifts greatly. They offered the same to Cortés, who was not as pleased because there was little gold, and what they did give was mixed with copper. This province was very large and had many markets, the biggest of which was in Nito, a neighborhood in the city of Itzamcamac.[104]

Some authors write that Quauhtemoc's death took place in Itzamcamac, but the natives' paintings, songs, and histories of this land—which are the ones I follow—tell it as I have written it.[105] In any

---

103. Carved gourds.

104. "Era esta provincia muy grande y tenía muchas ferias entre las cuales era la mayor la de Nito, barrio de por sí de la ciudad" (fol. 60r.). This confusing assertion is also revealing, since it stems from Alva Ixtlilxochitl's misconstruction of his source text, Gómara's *Historia de la conquista de México*. Gómara was actually referring to Pax-Bolon-Acha when he wrote, "tenía en muchos pueblos de ferias, como era Nito, factor y barrio por sí, poblado de sus vasallos y criados tratantes" (in many market towns such as Nito, Apoxpalon kept a commercial agent and a whole neighborhood where his trader vassals and servants lived; 1979, 334; our translation).

105. Gómara (1979, 336) states unequivocally that Cuauhtemoc was executed in "Izancanac."

case, they died somewhere in the province of Acalan, and Cortés killed them, though they were not guilty, so the land would be left without natural lords. If Cortés had realized the great good that God had done for him, he would have valued them as if they had been precious pearls; they were a testament to his achievements. Instead, he sought to kill the lords and even their children and obscure their deeds and keep all the glory for himself. Truth be told, it would have been impossible for him and his companions alone to conquer all the lands. The Spaniards hardly deserved so much credit, especially since Cortés had many more allies than enemies, and even those were hardly enemies because the Spaniards provoked them. Moreover, not only do the Spaniards minimize the help they received from those of Tezcuco, Tlaxcala, and other regions, but they shamelessly belittle the conquered beyond all truth and reason. The Spaniards have not followed the conventional wisdom. He who would enhance the glory and fame of the victory does not hesitate to praise the strength of the conquered for the greater glory and eternal triumph of the victor. If they were to do this it would only enhance their glory. It was truly a great thing that Cortés and the others who are called conquistadors did in establishing the law of the Gospel in this new world. If only they had not been so cruel, done the things mentioned in this and other histories, and done the things that follow.

God has allowed the native lords to fade from memory, and most of them have met an unfortunate end. As far as I know, Quauhtemoc and the others who died with him had been baptized and knew God. They lost their kingdoms and titles, but those are fleeting. God surely gave them the kingdom of heaven, which to us is more important than any fame or riches or worldly things. It may well please God to take away many of the seats[106] reserved for the first Spaniards who came to this land and give them to their native victims, even to some natives who are still living, because of their great misery. I have read many authors who write about the tyrannies and cruel-ties of other nations. All of them together do not compare with the great hardships and servitude of these natives. They themselves say they would rather be branded as slaves than live the way they now do. In this way the Spaniards who mistreat them would at least take pity on them to avoid damaging their property and lose their invest-

---

106. Places reserved in heaven.

ment. Their misfortune is so great that when a native trips and falls and gets hurt, the Spaniards draw indescribable pleasure from their suffering. As if this were not enough, they also hurl every insult that comes to mind at the injured native, and if the native dies the Spaniards say let the devil take them all. I say this because it happens all the time, and I have heard it said. But if God allows it, he knows why, and let us be thankful a thousand times over.

Later they left Itzamcamac and went to Mazatlan.[107] The journey took three days, during which they crossed some swamps and an estuary. Some of Ixtlilxochitl's soldiers went ahead, along with a prisoner from Mazatlan, who was a spy. A number of enemy warriors came out and took the prisoner. Angered by this, the soldiers fought valiantly until they took back the prisoner. One of the soldiers wounded the enemy captain in the arm, and he was seized and brought to Ixtlilxochitl, who took him as a guide. When they reached Mazatlan, they found no one there, because everyone had fled when they heard that the Spaniards were coming and how well the Aculhua fought. Ixtlilxochitl sent a merchant from Acalan to bring the lord governor of Mazatlan, who was a child, to him. The governor took them to Tiac, which is a day's journey from Mazatlan. At Tiac they were welcomed and entertained; the inhabitants refused to return to their houses and fled to a nearby hill. The next day they spent the night in Xuncahuitl, a well-fortified place. There were no people, but they found supplies and replenished their food stores for the five-day journey to Tiacac.[108] These places were abandoned because, according to the histories, word spread all over the land about the cruel death that Cortés inflicted on the kings and lords, and everyone was frightened because Ixtlilxochitl and his Aculhua vassals were still supporting Cortés and his companions. In light of this, those from these lands did as the people from Cohuatzacualco and other places had done. Every man and woman who heard that the Spaniards were coming abandoned their houses and fled out of fear and shock caused by the cruelties and tyrannies of the Spaniards,

---

107. The Nahuatl name for the Maya Kejach region, not to be confused with the city of Mazatlán in northern Mexico.

108. Taiça, from Tah Itza, the capital city of the Itza territory in the middle of Lake Petén Itza in northern Guatemala. In the next paragraph, Alva Ixtlilxochitl writes "Taicac," a misspelling that reflects Gómara (1979, 339). On the Itza, see Jones (1998).

especially when they saw what they did to people who were greater and more powerful than they were.

They walked for four days through deserted lands, and on the fifth day, after having climbed over a hill called Teteyztacan, they reached a great lake. In the middle of the lake was the capital city of the province of Taicac. They reached a place where there were many cultivated fields and some laborers, who, as soon as they saw the Spaniards, went onto the lake in the canoes they had there. The army had to work hard to reach this place, because they were walking in water up to their knees, and it was raining heavily. They had suffered this way throughout the journey. Along the way the guides seized a man. They sent him to Canec, the current lord of this province. On behalf of Ixtlilxochitl, he told Canec that they were coming to meet him with the children of the sun, who also wanted to see him and were ambassadors of the world's greatest lord. While this man carried out his task, Ixtlilxochitl set up and fortified his camp. Cortés did the same in the most suitable place they found, because this province was not known or subject to the Chichimeca Empire. The messenger returned at midnight with two nobles in the service of Canec. They spoke with Ixtlilxochitl and welcomed him and asked about his coming, the children of the sun, and the purpose of their journey. Ixtlilxochitl explained everything and sent for Canec, their lord, whom they wished to see. Ixtlilxochitl gave two captains in his service for them to keep as hostages. Cortés did the same by giving them a Spaniard. The next day Canec came with thirty nobles and brought with him the Spaniard and the two captains as well as some gifts, which he gave to Ixtlilxochitl and Cortés. Canec was greatly pleased to see the Spaniards. Ixtlilxochitl explained what they had come for and told him about matters of faith, which Canec was pleased to hear. He heard Mass, and the friars discussed the Mass and the mysteries of the faith with him. Canec promised to topple his idols and asked for a cross to place in his city. After this and much conversation, it was lunchtime, and he gave our forces bread, chicken, honey, and fish; he offered himself as an ally and a vassal of the emperor.[109] Then he took Cortés and Ixtlilxochitl and a number of Spaniards inside the city, where he burned the idols.

---

109. Grant Jones (1998, 35) speculates that Ahau Canek's attitude was designed to avoid conflict and dismiss the Spaniards as quickly as possible. The Itza managed to avoid Spanish impositions until the late seventeenth century.

Meanwhile, the army began marching on, and since it was late, Cortés and Ixtlilxochitl departed with some guides to follow the Spaniards and native allies that had previously passed through this city. They reached the army, which had gone beyond the lake, and they spent the night on a nearby field. The next day they continued their journey across level ground, where they killed a number of deer—of which there are an infinite number in those parts. They met some hunters who were carrying a dead lion.[110] They captured them and used them as guides, along with those from Taicac, until they reached a very large and deep estuary, across from which was the town where they were headed. The people in this place, seeing the Spaniards, began to abandon their houses taking their belongings, women, and children. Two local natives riding in a canoe with a maiden were seized. These men guided the army to a place where they could cross, which was one league away. Once there, they resupplied themselves with all that they needed and satisfied their hunger. They spent four days waiting for Amoan, the lord of Tlezcan, which is the name of this place. The lord Amoan never came, and neither did his vassals. And so our army left, after taking enough supplies for a six-day journey. On the first day they stayed in an inn belonging to Amoan, which was six leagues from Tlezcan. They spent a day there, celebrated the feast of Our Lady, and fished in a nearby river. They caught a good number of tasty fish. On the next day's journey they killed some deer, and after walking across some level ground, they traversed a mountain pass, walking up and down slopes for four leagues. It grew dark when they reached the foot of the mountain, and here they spent the night. They rested for a day, and the next day they walked to a small town belonging to Amoan called Axuncapuyn, where they spent two days. Then, on the next day, they walked to Taxaytetl, where they slept. This town also belonged to Amoan, and there they found great quantities of food and refreshment and men who told them where to go.

The next day they started their journey, and having gone two leagues, they came to a tall mountain range. It took them eight days to climb eight leagues, and they suffered much hardship from unrelenting rain, hunger, and misery. Sixty-some horses died after falling from cliffs and breaking their legs. A nephew of Cortés also fell from

---

110. Not an African lion, but a generic term for a large wild cat.

a cliff and broke his leg in three or four places, and the natives pulled him out with great effort. Beyond this mountain range, they came to a large and fast-flowing river. Ixtlilxochitl sent runners to find out if there was a place where the river narrowed upstream. The runners soon came back and said that they had found a rock, naturally situated over the river, that could be easily crossed as if it were a bridge. The Spaniards were greatly pleased with the news because they were growing desperate. This was at Easter time, and they had all confessed, imagining they would soon die. Once on the rock, they used some logs to bridge a gap and reach the other side. Once they were across, they slept in a town nearby called Teoxic. They found some people but very little food, and they were very hungry, especially the natives who had been surviving on plants during all these challenging days. The food they had brought from Taxaytetl had run out. The people of this place told our forces that a province called Tahuican lay at a one-day journey upriver and that they would find many supplies and everything they needed there. However, it was on the other side of the river. Ixtlilxochitl sent more than one thousand Aculhua vassals with some Spaniards to bring supplies. This company crossed the river and provided food for the army many times, though at a great cost.

While they were in this place, they sent some Aculhua and some Spaniards, along with a guide, to another province called Azuculin. After a few leagues this company came to an inn, where they found seven men and one woman. They found out from them that the road was flat and good all the way to Azuculin, and a native from Acalan provided further information about everything. They spent a few days here, then they left for Azuculin without any guides, because the guide from Acalan and the others fled one night. They walked for three days on a bad road until they finally reached Azuculin, which was abandoned, and they did not find any supplies and suffered great need and hunger. For over eight days they looked for someone to guide them to Nito, but no one was ever found. Looking closely at the painted map that showed where they had to go, they found that they were not far from some places subject to the province of Tunia. As they were going on their way, they found a youth, whom they seized, and he guided them through some hills to some small villages in the province. It took two days to get there, but when they arrived, they found everything abandoned except for an old man, who guided them for two days. They reached a town where they seized four men, who were the only ones there, because the rest had fled and abandoned their houses. Ixtlilxochitl asked them if they knew how far it was to Nito. They responded that it was two days' journey from here. To gain further assurance about the information provided, he released two of them and ordered them to go and bring back some people to confirm that. They brought back two women from Nito, who explained where it was and that there were some Spaniards who were already there. Cortés was not satisfied. He sent some Spaniards to confirm that there were Spaniards at that place. This group went and seized some men and came back to tell Cortés.

Once the information was confirmed, Cortés then wrote to Diego Nieto, who was the captain, to request rafts to cross the river. They marched on with the army. They spent five days on the road and crossed the river at Tunia, where the Aculhua suffered great hunger. Once they arrived in Nito, they found even less to eat, because the Spaniards who were there were sick and famished. Ixtlilxochitl divided up the soldiers, sending some to look for plants to eat and others around to the neighboring towns to see if they could find some supplies. They found nothing but cruel battles with the natives, though in Lequela, which is a two-day journey from Nito, Ixtlilxochitl's men were able to bring back some supplies. Seeing their need, Cortés asked Ixtlilxochitl to go with him to the Bay of San Andrés on three ships that he had readied. They took sixty of Ixtlilxochitl's Aculhua vassals, the most skilled and courageous, as well as forty Spaniards selected for this journey. Meanwhile, the army went on foot to Naco, a three-day journey from this place, with Gonzalo de Sandoval and the rest of the Spaniards. They were to join up with Cortés's party in Naco and pacify the Spaniards there, who were in revolt.

After Cortés left, they traveled a few days until they reached a gulf that measures over thirty leagues, according to the Spanish historians. Then Cortés and Ixtlilxochitl went ashore, each with nearly thirty soldiers. They reached a place that was abandoned and in ruins, where they took some maize and chili peppers before returning to their boats. Then they proceeded on their way, and there was a storm. One of Ixtlilxochitl's soldiers, who was a native of Tezcuco, was riding in a canoe and drowned. They reached the river and left some Spaniards and natives in the canoes and brigantines; the rest

went with Cortés and Ixtlilxochitl. After a short time, they reached
another abandoned town. Then they climbed some mountains with
much difficulty until they came to some cultivated fields, where they
found one man and three women in a small hut. The man guided
them to another house, where they took two women, and from here
they went to a very small town that was also abandoned. There were
many chickens and other birds but no maize or salt, which is what
they were looking for. They had been inside a certain house for a
while when the inhabitants came back without knowing anyone
was there. The residents were seized. These people guided our forces
along a very difficult road through the mountains and across many
rivers flowing down from the mountains.

They reached a town where, because there were many people,
our forces did not enter. They slept uncomfortably here because of
heavy rainfall, thunder and lighting, and many mosquitos. As soon
as it dawned, they entered the sleeping town and found many people
asleep in the houses of the town's lord. The Spaniards fell upon
them and killed more than fifteen. They also seized fifteen men and
twenty-some women. With such signs of friendship, obviously these
towns were going to be abandoned! The prisoners guided them to
another, bigger town, which they said had maize and all the supplies that they had not found here. On the way they captured eight
hunters and some woodcutters. After they crossed a great river with
much effort, they reached a field, where they slept. At midnight the
inhabitants of the nearby town, hearing the Spaniards, roused their
warriors, lit many fires, and sounded their instruments. Ixtlilxochitl
told Cortés that before anything else happened they should enter the
town and quickly defeat it or else leave, because they were in great
peril. Cortés said that it would be better to attack them and take them
unawares. So this was done. They entered the town and killed many
people and barricaded themselves into the square. The inhabitants
fled. At dawn they found no one. Then they plundered the houses,
where they found many blankets, cotton, maize, salt, and other
things. They also found much fruit, chickens and other birds, chili
peppers, and cacao beans.

The ships were a three-day journey away from this place, along
a very difficult route. The river that runs through this town flows
to the place where the boats were, so they called for the brigantines and canoes to be brought and loaded with food and provisions.

Meanwhile, the natives of Tezcuco were ordered by Cortés to build four rafts, so they could also carry the maize. The current was too strong for the brigantine and canoes to go all the way upriver to the town. So they used the rafts to take the supplies, which was difficult and dangerous, because the natives on both sides of the river shot many arrows and stones. No one died, although Ixtlilxochitl and Cortés and the rest were wounded; the people who went by land did not face any dangers. As they continued on the river, they supplied their boats and brigantines in other towns and places that they found. After one day and one night they reached the gulf. Once everyone was aboard the ships, they returned to Nito. According to the histories, this journey took thirty-five days.

When they arrived in Nito, Cortés gathered the remaining Spaniards and those of Gil González and set out for San Andrés Bay, where Ixtlilxochitl's army and Spaniards were waiting. They were in this port for twenty days, and after leaving some people there, they went to the Port of Honduras. They spent nine days sailing, after which they landed and went ashore. Two days later Ixtlilxochitl sent two of his soldiers with a Spaniard sent by Cortés to two provincial capitals called Chapaxina and Papayca, which were a day's journey from this place. They were to tell them that Ixtlilxochitl had come with Captain Cortés and to ask them to come see him to discuss certain matters. The lords of this province were very pleased with the news and quickly sent their messengers along with Ixtlilxochitl's envoys to welcome him. After the messengers heard Ixtlilxochitl's explanation of Cortés's mission, they returned to their lords.

Five days later two nobles arrived with much maize, chicken, and food sent on behalf of their lords. They wanted to hear firsthand what Ixtlilxochitl wanted and why Cortés had come. The lords wondered why they were being summoned and begged their pardon. But they did not dare come, because they had already received a thousand insults from Spaniards, who had come to abduct men and force them onto their ships. Speaking through Marina,[111] Ixtlilxochitl told Cortés

---

111. This is the only instance in this text where Alva Ixtlilxochitl mentions doña Marina, also known as Malinche, by name; the act of interpreting occurs only two other times in the text. The absence of intermediaries creates the impression of perfect understanding between Cortés and his great friend Ixtlilxochitl. Likewise, in his second letter Cortés refers only once to the "Indian woman from Putunchan" (1986, 73) who served as his interpreter. On doña Marina's symbolic significance, see Cypess (1991).

everything that these lords had said. Cortés asked Ixtlilxochitl to reassure the nobles and explain more clearly the reason they had come. Cortés also asked Ixtlilxochitl to send the nobles to bring the lords to them so that he could set them at ease. Ixtlilxochitl sent the nobles with messages explaining in detail why they had come and with a request for them to come meet him. He told them they should not be afraid, because the Spaniards would not harm them and were their friends. He also requested that they send supplies for his army, which was in great need of them, as well as a number of laborers and woodcutters to fell trees from a hilltop, which Cortés thought was necessary. Having heard what Ixtlilxochitl requested, the lords quickly gathered as many people as they could for this purpose and came to meet him, bringing many supplies. They cleared the hilltop.

In the midst of all this coming and going, and as many other things that would take too long to recount were happening, Cortés received news from Cuba about the revolts that were taking place in Mexico.[112] In light of this, Cortés tried three or four times to set sail, but he was not able to because of the bad weather. He had to content himself with sending Martín Dorantes to Pánuco with letters. Cortés also requested that Ixtlilxochitl send nobles from Tezcuco, Mexico, and Tlacopan to order Ixtlilxochitl's governors to quell any unrest that could spark widespread rebellion and cause much violence and death. Dorantes managed to reach his destination, though it was not easy. The lords and nobles sent by Ixtlilxochitl found the land quiet and peaceful, except for the Spaniards, who, as we have said before, were mired in discord.

Once Cortés had sent off Dorantes, Ixtlilxochitl sent some soldiers, led by his friend Chichinquatzin to explore the land with Hernando de Sayavedra, who took sixty Spaniards with him. This company traveled through a valley, encountering many lands, towns, and fertile places. Chichinquatzin was so skillful that he won over many towns as allies without the Spaniards having to suffer any grief or hardship. Twenty lords came to meet Ixtlilxochitl and offer their alliance, subjects, and vassals to Cortés and the rest of the Spaniards.

112. The infighting among the Spaniards mentioned earlier. The news came from Alonso Zuazo, who had been shipped off to Cuba by Gonzalo de Salazar (Porras Muñoz 1978, 371).

They also provided everything that was needed to sustain Ixtlilxochitl's army and the Spaniards.

The lords of the provinces of Papayca and Chapaxina began to distance themselves. Although they still came to Ixtlilxochitl, they did so less willingly than before. They were upset by things that the Spaniards had done to them. Ixtlilxochitl requested that they surrender, but they would not listen to his messengers, so he sent some of his soldiers who were able to capture them. They brought three lords. The first was called Chicueytl, the second Pochotl, and the third Mendereto. They were brought before Ixtlilxochitl, who delivered them to Cortés. They say Cortés had them shackled and told them he would not release them until they surrendered and ordered their people to return to their towns. The lords sent word for their vassals to return to their homes and surrender if they wanted to see their lords alive and free. Seeing the dire straights their lords were in, the people of Chapaxina quickly surrendered and returned to their towns. As a result, the lords were released, after promising Ixtlilxochitl that they would never again rebel and that they would always be allies of Cortés and the other Spaniards.

However, those from Papayca would not surrender. Ixtlilxochitl sent some of his vassals to conquer them, along with some Spaniards sent by Cortés. One night they entered the city and captured three governors, or tutors, of the local lord, who was a child. These men had usurped the young lord's throne. The most powerful of them was named Pizacura. Once they were caught they were taken with the rest of the plunder to Truxillo,[113] which is what Cortés named this place. Pizacura made excuses, saying that he had no part in this rebellion, but that Matzal, who was the most powerful of them, had incited it. Pizacura asked to be released, saying that he would deliver Matzal to the Christians. He was released, but he did not fulfill his promise. Therefore, Ixtlilxochitl ordered that Matzal be captured. When Matzal was brought to him, he delivered him to Cortés, who had him hanged because he would not surrender, though they say he very much wanted to surrender and that his vassals prevented him from doing so. Then they marched on Papayca and mercilessly defeated it. They captured Pizacura a second time, along with the

113. Truxillo, Honduras.

youth who was the true lord, as I have said. And with this, the entire region was defeated and pacified.

Cortés gave the order to move toward the province of Huictlato and Nicarahua. According to the historians, as he was readying himself to go, Cortés's cousin, fray Diego Altamirano, came and told him everything that had happened in Mexico and that it was on the verge of being lost because of Spanish infighting. Cortés asked Ixtlilxochitl to send a number of his vassals ahead to prepare the road through Quauhtemalan by which he intended to go. Ixtlilxochitl did as requested and sent some Aculhua and some natives from Honduras for this purpose. However, in the end, Cortés did not go by land. The forces sent by Ixtlilxochitl were informed that Cortés would go by sea. They continued on their journey without waiting any longer. They took the same route that had been used by most of the army a few days before. The army had been in Naco, as Cortés and Ixtlilxochitl had commanded, and was led by Gonzalo de Sandoval. Some authors claim that Ixtlilxochitl was with the people who were supposed to prepare the road, but popular opinion holds that he was always with Cortés and therefore did not go by land. Ixtlilxochitl sent word to all the cities, towns, and places to prepare the roads with everything necessary. The natives did this with great joy, for they could not wait to see their lord.

Of all the kings and princes and great lords who went with Cortés, only Ixtlilxochitl came back alive. The towns that Cortés had founded, one called Truxillo and the other Natividad, were organized, and two ships were prepared and supplied for voyage. Cortés set sail with twenty Spaniards and Ixtlilxochitl with two hundred soldiers and many lords from those parts. They left from the Port of Truxillo in the year eight *toxtli*,[114] on the sixteenth day of the month of *tozoztzintli*,[115] which is according to our calendar April 25, 1526. Because of the bad weather, they ended up in Cuba, where they spent, so they say, ten days. Eight days after they left Cuba, they arrived in Chalchicoeca, where they went ashore. Then they spent eight days in Medellín. Ixtlilxochitl sent word of his arrival, after a long and arduous journey, to Tezcuco, Mexico, Tacuba, and other places. Everyone was greatly pleased by his return, and it brought

---

114. 8 Rabbit.
115. Little Vigil.

them great solace, although they were very saddened by the news of
the deaths of their kings and lords. They set out for Mexico. All along
the way they were received with great ceremony. The lords came out
to greet them, not only those from nearby, but also some from as far
as seventy or eighty leagues away. They came bearing rich gifts for
Ixtlilxochitl, since they had no one else to show their allegiance to.
They also brought gifts for Cortés and the rest of his companions.
Wherever Ixtlilxochitl went, the lords consoled him and wept along
with him for his efforts and toil and for the death of their kings
and lords. It was a sad thing to see. As the songs tell, the lords were
like children who had lost their parents, for that is what it felt like.
Fourteen days later they reached the city of Tezcuco, their beloved
homeland. There was great rejoicing by Ixtlilxochitl's kinsmen and
vassals. The next day Cortés and the rest of the Spaniards left for
Mexico, where he was well received.

This was the end of the long journey that Ixtlilxochitl made to
Yhueras. He traveled more than five hundred leagues, according to
the Spanish authors, especially Gómara, who agrees with my history
in terms of the places they went and the time it took them to travel.
I have not dealt with those they call conquistadors, because they
are not part of my story. Moreover, many historians have remembered them and have forgotten Ixtlilxochitl and his vassals. Also, the
paintings, which I follow, do not tell of the Spaniards, except in those
parts where I make note of it. This journey was one of the greatest
hardships endured by any prince in this new world. Ixtlilxochitl's
suffering was perhaps greater than any experienced by his ancestors,
except for Topiltzin, the last king of the Tolteca. He suffered almost as
greatly and confronted similar adversities, according to the histories.
Xolotl journeyed far, but he did not suffer as much as Ixtlilxochitl.[116]
Ixtlilxochitl's grandfather, Nezahualcoyotl, also suffered greatly and
journeyed for many years, but this was always within his homeland.
It seems to me that Ixtlilxochitl was a second Topiltzin,[117] who wan-
dered, suffered hardship, and under whom the Tolteca Empire was

116. As noted earlier, Xolotl was the first Gran Chichimeca and a direct ancestor of
Ixtlilxochitl.

117. According to Alva Ixtlilxochitl (1975–77, 2:12), Topiltzin was the last ruler of
the great Tolteca Empire, which after 572 years of ascendancy was wrecked by famine,
disease, and internal strife. Topiltzin was also a forebear of Ixtlilxochitl. On the role of
genealogy in Alva Ixtlilxochitl's works, see García Loaeza (2014b).

irreparably destroyed after 572 years. The same has happened with Ixtlilxochitl. His death marked the end of the southern Chichimeca Empire,[118] which lasted just as long.

There were other expeditions to different regions, besides those recounted here, that I do not include, in order to avoid verbosity. There were expeditions to Colima and Hueimolan and other parts. There was also one to Tlapalan, which is one of the provinces that lay in the general direction of Yhueras, and in which Ixtlilxochitl personally participated, according to the songs and paintings. On this journey, as in all others that Ixtlilxochitl was on, he sent a large number of forces to support the Christians, according to the histories and many accounts that I have in my possession from don Alonso Axayaca and other authors. Besides what is told in the histories, this has been confirmed in conversations I have heard among old men, since some who witnessed these events are still alive. They say the smallest army from Tezcuco that went to the aforementioned places had more than five thousand soldiers. Ixtlilxochitl always provided all they needed, including supplies, clothes, weapons, and many other necessities. He also gave them very generous rewards, according to the ancient custom, which he paid for with a large portion of his family's wealth and treasure, all the tribute from his father's and grandfather's warehouses and the tribute rendered daily by his vassals and other kingdoms and provinces subject to the three capitals. He also spent all the gold and precious stones that he had and those of other lords who were his friends and kinsmen.

Cortés and the others eagerly asked for this treasure, in keeping with their voracious greed and avarice. That is the problem with greedy people: the more you give them, the more they want, and they are never satisfied. This is clear in the histories written by various authors. Even the unfortunate soldiers not only shared their rewards with the Christians but gave them everything they had to keep them contented. As it is written in the histories and is also well known, the first Christians who came to this land claim the triumph of victory for themselves, but the native soldiers carried most of the

118.   In the *Compendio histórico del reino de Texcoco*, Alva Ixtlilxochitl (1975–77, 1:422), locates the original Chichimeca Empire somewhere in the northern reaches of New Spain. The Southern Chichimeca Empire was established by the Chichimeca prince Xolotl in the tenth century, when he claimed the territory of the fallen Tolteca Empire for himself and his descendants.

burden, as the humble and hard-working people[119] that they were. In sum, Ixtlilxochitl spent large and excessive amounts in the conquests, or conversion, of this land, as we have seen, and this was no small service to God and His Majesty the emperor. Ixtlilxochitl was left poor and unrewarded. To this day his descendants can rely only on God's shelter and on the clemency of our lord King Philip III.[120]

Ixtlilxochitl was told about everything that had happened since he left for Yhueras. He also received reports about his three governors, or viceroys—Itzcuincuani from Tezcuco, Mexicaltecuhtli from Mexico, and Contecatl from Tlacopan—along with the other governors from the subject provinces. Ixtlilxochitl suffered great sadness because of their poor performance. According to some authors, they had been complicit with the Spaniards in the deaths of princes and many important nobles from Tezcuco, Mexico, Tlacopan, and the other places. Some of these lords had been Ixtlilxochitl's brothers and kinsmen, and the governors had abused them by using them as slaves. Other lords were in hiding in foreign lands, leaving their houses and homeland, all for fear of dying. They knew from others' experiences that they would be killed for no reason. Some left to avoid the shame of having to serve these villains, who had been their vassals.

In fact, the governors had not obeyed Ixtlilxochitl's orders and had been so tyrannical that, besides everything else, they had stolen what little there was in the palaces of Ixtlilxochitl and his kinsmen, spent all the tribute collected while he was in Yhueras, and humiliated the natives in a thousand different ways. The governors built houses for the Spaniards in Mexico City on lands that belonged to Ixtlilxochitl and the other lords, and they had practically given them away—for a hat, a pair of shoes, and items of lesser value. And for any piece of Spanish woolen clothing, they would have given a lot more. The state of affairs was such that when Ixtlilxochitl found out, he was shocked and outraged by these tyrant governors. He decided not to do anything, not even to inform them that he had returned—though they were well aware—until he saw what might happen. The nobles

---

119. Alva Ixtlilxochitl's original Spanish reads, "gente de pan y naranja, o, por mejor decir, carne de vaca" (CC INAH, vol. 2, fol. 66v–67r). This phrase was particularly challenging to decipher. Our English translation is not literal but rather reflects our understanding of the intent of the idiomatic expression within the context of the sentence.

120. Reigned 1598–1621.

came every day to see Ixtlilxochitl, bringing a thousand complaints, telling him that they were made to pay tribute and were sent to serve the Spaniards. Itzcuincuani, the most powerful of the three governors, was most to blame. He further insulted them by calling them *pilçoltin*, which means low-ranking noble or gentlemen. Iztcuincuani said that all that was over and that now people like himself and the Spaniards were the lords of the land, which is what Cortés and his companions were saying.

Ixtlilxochitl was so distraught when he learned about this that he immediately ordered all the remaining nobles and lords to take a *huacal*[121] and carry the building materials for the Franciscan temple and the cathedral in Mexico. Ixtlilxochitl, as their leader, was the first to pick up a big huacal, made from a tiger's[122] hide, that was full of stone. He led the nobles to Mexico laden with stone, lime, and sand. Others followed them, pulling wood. Ixtlilxochitl told them to be patient and show courage so that the traitorous upstarts would see that, though it was not their trade, the nobles could do the work without help from the traitors. He also told them to do this in order to be an example to their vassals, the commoners, and to strengthen the resolve of those who would follow them in this service of building God's church. As leaders, it was their duty to be the first in building God's temples. Ixtlilxochitl wanted to be the first in all things as long as he lived to serve as an example for his vassals. He had been the first to be baptized and first to serve God and the emperor in battle in support of the Christians. He had also been the first to work on the rebuilding of Mexico, as we have seen. Seeing the zeal and courage of this exceptional prince, the nobles were happy when they reached Mexico, though tired from hauling their heavy loads, which were twice as heavy as what the commoners could carry. Loaded as they were, they went straight to the place that Ixtlilxochitl had designated years ago for the Franciscan Church of San José and the cathedral. The friary was nearly complete, so they began work on the church. In those days, the Mass was said beneath a very tall cross, which stood until just a few years ago.

Once the new Franciscan church was almost finished, and seeing that the work was progressing, Ixtlilxochitl returned to the city of

121. A basket for carrying goods on a person's back.
122. A generic term for a large wild cat.

Tezcuco, leaving the rest of the nobles behind, so it would be easier
to send them building materials and provide them everything that
was needed. While he was in Mexico, Ixtlilxochitl, the great captain and lord of all the land, was willing to work as a mason. And
the whole time he was in Mexico, the governors did not deign to
see him or help him, as they were very set in their misguided ways
and interested only in pleasing the Spaniards. This did not displease
Ixtlilxochitl, who was only waiting for a better time to punish them
in accordance with their guilt. Once in Tezcuco Ixtlilxochitl continued
to send everything that was needed and supported the friars, who
consoled him and were very happy with his good company. The friars
had suffered much hardship and harassment from the Spaniards,
because they defended the natives and pitied them and their calamities. The native witnesses, some of whom are still alive today, say
that it came to the point where a large number of Ixtlilxochitl's men
guarded the friars night and day so that they would not be harmed
by the Spaniards. I find this shocking, but it is common knowledge,
and that is why I write about it here. The first Spaniards who came to
this land committed so many misdeeds of this sort that it would take
too long to recount them all here. I also do not want people to say
that I write more than is warranted. Suffice it to say that what I say
here is nothing compared to what I could say.

If the Spanish chroniclers have failed to recount these misdeeds,
it must be because they got their accounts from those who committed them and for the sake of their honor did not want to speak about
it. Or, if someone did mention them, he was not believed. If the first
founders of the law of the Gospel[123] did not leave an account of these
affronts, it is because they were the blessed servants of God, who
led holy and praiseworthy lives, bore these affronts for the love of
God, and paid the Spaniards no heed. Nevertheless, I believe that
what I say is well known by the friars that live to this day at the
Franciscan church, and some of them will find it written by those
who saw it or will have heard about it from those who witnessed it,
because it happened only a few years ago. But in the end, whether
they are recorded by the Spaniards or not, these misdeeds are well
documented. It is shown in the paintings and it is written that in
those times many natives guarded the places where the friars lived,

123. That is, the friars.

including Tezcuco, Mexico, Tlacopan, Xochimilco, and Tlaxcala; they set watchmen at night as if they were in enemy territory. All this is further proof that the Spaniards lied when they said that the lords Quauhtemoc, Cohuanacoch, Tetlepanquetzal, and the rest wanted to rise up against them while they were in Yhueras or Acalan. This was clearly a false account. None of these lords held power at the time; upstart lackeys held it instead. These upstarts were quick to side with the Spaniards and follow their commands, and they scorned their natural lords. This was the cause of much tyranny.

Epilogue

For the seventeenth-century author of the "Thirteenth Relation,"
don Fernando de Alva Ixtlilxochitl, the history of the conquest of
Mexico elicited two contradictory emotions. On the one hand, he felt
joy at the arrival of the law of the Gospel, which he saw as offering spiritual salvation to his native ancestors. On the other hand,
however, he felt an acute sense of loss and offense, as the Spaniards
destabilized the rigid social hierarchies of central Mexico and preconquest lords such as Ixtlilxochitl struggled to maintain their authority
in the postconquest landscape. As he noted in the concluding lines of
another work, *Sumaria relación de la Nueva España* [Summary relation of New Spain], Alva Ixtlilxochitl felt it a great injustice that the
people who in pre-Hispanic times were *macehuales*, or commoners,
and the underlings of his illustrious ancestors became accustomed
to being addressed as gentlemen, while the "sons and daughters,
granddaughters and relatives of Nezahualcoyotl and Nezahualpilli go
about ploughing and digging just to have enough to eat" (1975–77,
1:392–93; our translation). It is unlikely that don Fernando Cortés
Ixtlilxochitl, who lived for only about a decade into the colonial
period, was forced to work his own fields, but the conquest undoubtedly set in motion substantial shifts in the indigenous social order.

Unfortunately, we know little of what happened to Ixtlilxochitl
after the conquest. Alva Ixtlilxochitl's accounts do not go beyond
the events described at the end of the "Thirteenth Relation," and
Ixtlilxochitl does not figure prominently in very many archival

documents or in any other postconquest histories.[1] Ixtlilxochitl is also absent from Mexico's national pantheon of heroes because of his alliance with the Spaniards, which later generations of Mexican intellectuals came to regard as traitorous. For example, Carlos María de Bustamante, a foremost advocate of Mexican independence, scathingly condemns Ixtlilxochitl in the prologue to his 1829 edition of the "Thirteenth Relation." After detailing Ixtlilxochitl's perceived betrayals, Bustamante asked rhetorically, "Who then would not see in Ixtlilxochitl one of the greatest enemies of his country?" (xxi; our translation).

Modern scholars have been a bit more generous in their appraisals of Ixtlilxochitl. Frederic Hicks cast Ixtlilxochitl as a pragmatist, noting that "loyal allies of a victorious lord could expect to be rewarded, with lands, vassals, and perhaps political posts, as well as material gifts, while defeated enemies would be lucky to escape with their lives" (1994, 236). Ixtlilxochitl's decision to ally himself with the Spaniards, then, was an opportunity to advance, perhaps, or at least not to be killed. It was part of the ongoing process of adaptation and negotiation that native leaders and commoners had been engaged in from the moment of contact, and one in which they would continue to participate for centuries.

Indeed, Tetzcoco's native nobles proved remarkably resilient in the decades and centuries following the conquest. Admittedly, there were some significant setbacks, such as the death of don Carlos Ometochtli, one of Ixtlilxochitl's half brothers, who was accused by the Inquisition of encouraging native people to return to their pre-Christian religious practices. Don Carlos was tried, found guilty, and burned at the stake in 1539.[2] But there were many successes also. Descendants of Tetzcoco's pre-Hispanic rulers gradually reasserted their social and political dominance over the course of the sixteenth century. And as late as the nineteenth century—even after Mexico declared its independence from Spain—the family continued to possess aristocratic titles and a large lordly estate.[3] As don Fernando de Alva Ixtlilxochitl's work here has shown, the Spanish conquest

---

1. Ixtlilxochitl does appear in the *Códice Ramírez* (1979). However, that text does not add any additional information about his life or activities after the period covered by the "Thirteenth Relation."

2. AGN-Inq (2:10). See also González Obregón (1910).

3. AGN-T (3594:2, fol. 1r–54v).

was hardly a "Spanish" conquest. The inclination to impose a tidy Spanish-versus-Indian division on these events is plainly wrong. Ever present alongside the Spanish conquerors, and present in far greater numbers, were native conquistadors.

REFERENCES

Acosta, José de. 2002. *Natural and Moral History of the Indies.* Edited by
    Jane E. Mangan. Translated by Frances M. López-Morillas. Durham:
    Duke University Press.
Adorno, Rolena. 1997. "History, Law, and the Eyewitness Protocols of
    Authority in Bernal Díaz del Castillo's *Historia verdadera de la con-*
    quista de la Nueva España." In *The Project of Prose in Early Modern*
    Europe and the New World, edited by Elizabeth Fowler and Roland
    Greene, 154–75. Cambridge: Cambridge University Press.
———. 2007. *The Polemics of Possession in Spanish American Narrative.*
    New Haven: Yale University Press.
———. 2011. *Colonial Latin American Literature: A Very Short Introduc-*
    tion. Oxford: Oxford University Press.
Aguilar-Moreno, Manuel. 2006. *Handbook to Life in the Aztec World.*
    Oxford: Oxford University Press.
Altman, Ida. 2010. *The War for Mexico's West: Indians and Spaniards in*
    New Galicia, 1524–1550. Albuquerque: University of New Mexico
    Press.
Alva, Bartolomé de. 1999. *A Guide to Confession Large and Small in*
    the Mexican Language, 1634. Edited by Barry D. Sell and John F.
    Schwaller. Norman: University of Oklahoma Press.
Alva Ixtlilxochitl, Fernando de. 1969. *Ally of Cortés: Account 13, Of the*
    Coming of the Spaniards and the Beginning of the Evangelical Law.
    Translated by Douglass Ballantine. El Paso: Texas Western Press.
———. 1975–77. *Obras históricas.* Edited by Edmundo O'Gorman. 2 vols.
    Mexico City: Instituto de Investigaciones Históricas, Universidad
    Nacional Autónoma de México.
Anderson, Arthur J. O., Frances Berdan, and James Lockhart. 1976. *Beyond*
    the Codices: The Nahua View of Colonial Mexico. Berkeley: Univer-
    sity of California Press.
Anderson, Arthur J. O., and Charles E. Dibble, trans. 1950–82. *The Florentine*
    Codex: General History of the Things of New Spain. 13 parts. Salt
    Lake City: University of Utah Press; Santa Fe: School of American
    Research.

Asselbergs, Florine G. L. 2008. *Conquered Conquistadors: The Lienzo de Quauhquechollan; A Nahua Vision of the Conquest of Guatemala*. Boulder: University Press of Colorado.

Ballentine, Douglass K. 1969. *Ally of Cortés: Account 13, of the Coming of the Spaniards and the Beginning of the Evangelical Law*. El Paso: Texas Western Press.

Barlow, Robert H. 1945. "Some Remarks on the Term 'Aztec Empire.'" *Americas* 1 (3): 345–49.

Benton, Bradley. 2014. "The Outsider: Alva Ixtlilxochitl's Tenuous Ties to the City of Tetzcoco." *Colonial Latin American Review* 23 (1): 37–52.

Boone, Elizabeth Hill. 2000. *Stories in Red and Black: Pictorial Histories of the Aztecs and Mixtecs*. Austin: University of Texas Press.

Brading, David A. 1991. *The First America: The Spanish Monarchy, Creole Patriots, and the Liberal State, 1492–1867*. Cambridge: Cambridge University Press.

Brian, Amber. 2010. "Don Fernando de Alva Ixtlilxochitl's Narratives of the Conquest of Mexico: Colonial Subjectivity and the Circulation of Native Knowledge." In Schroeder 2010b, 124–43.

———. 2014a. "The Alva Ixtlilxochitl Brothers and the Nahua Intellectual Community." In Lee and Brokaw 2014, 201–18.

———. 2014b. "The Original Alva Ixtlilxochitl Manuscripts at Cambridge University." *Colonial Latin American Review* 23 (1): 84–101.

Burkhart, Louise. 1989. *The Slippery Earth: Nahua-Christian Moral Dialogue in Sixteenth- Century Mexico*. Tucson: University of Arizona Press.

Bustamante, Carlos María de, ed. 1829. *Horribles crueldades de los conquistadores de México y de los indios que los auxiliaron para subyugarlo a la corona de Castilla: Ó sea memoria escrita por D. Fernando de Alva Ixtlilxuchitl*. México: Alejandro Valdés.

Carrasco, Pedro. 1999. *The Tenochca Empire of Ancient Mexico: The Triple Alliance of Tenochtitlan, Tetzcoco, and Tlacopan*. Norman: University of Oklahoma Press.

Chamberlain, Robert S. 1939. "The Concept of *Señor Natural* as Revealed by Castilian Law and Administrative Documents." *Hispanic American Historical Review* 19:130–37.

Chimalpahin Quauhtlehuanitzin, don Domingo de San Antón Muñón. 1997. *Codex Chimalpahin*. Edited and translated by Arthur J. O. Anderson and Susan Schroeder. 2 vols. Norman: University of Oklahoma Press.

Clendinnen, Inga. 1987. *Ambivalent Conquests: Maya and Spaniard in Yucatan, 1517–1570*. Cambridge: Cambridge University Press.

Códice Ramírez. 1979. Mexico City: Editorial Innovación.

Cook, Noble David. 1998. *Born to Die: Disease and New World Conquest, 1492–1650*. Cambridge: Cambridge University Press.

Cortés, Hernán. 1986. *Letters from Mexico*. Edited and translated by Anthony Pagden. New Haven: Yale University Press.

Cypess, Sandra Messinger. 1991. *La Malinche in Mexican Literature from History to Myth*. Austin: University of Texas Press.

Díaz del Castillo, Bernal. 2009. *The True History of the Conquest of New Spain*. Edited by David Carrasco. Albuquerque: University of New Mexico Press.

Diel, Lori Boornazian. 2008. *The Tira de Tepechpan: Negotiating Place Under Aztec and Spanish Rule*. Austin: University of Texas Press.

Durán, Diego. 1994. *The History of the Indies of New Spain*. Translated by Doris Heyden. Norman: University of Oklahoma Press.

Elliot, John H. 1986. "Cortés, Velázquez, and Charles V." In Cortés 1986, xi–xxxvii.

Farriss, Nancy M. 1984. *Maya Society Under Colonial Rule: The Collective Enterprise of Survival*. Princeton: Princeton University Press.

García Loaeza, Pablo. 2014a. "Deeds to Be Praised for All Time: Alva Ixtlilxochitl's *Historia de la nación chichimeca* and Geoffrey of Monmouth's *History of the Kings of Britain*." *Colonial Latin American Review* 23 (1): 53–69.

———. 2014b. "Fernando de Alva Ixtlilxochitl's Texcocan Dynasty: Nobility, Genealogy, and Historiography." In Lee and Brokaw 2014, 219–42.

Gerhard, Peter. 1972. *A Guide to the Historical Geography of New Spain*. Norman: University of Oklahoma Press, 1993.

Gibson, Charles. 1952. *Tlaxcala in the Sixteenth Century*. Stanford: Stanford University Press, 1967.

———. 1964. *The Aztecs Under Spanish Rule: A History of the Indians of the Valley of Mexico, 1519–1810*. Stanford: Stanford University Press.

Gómara, Francisco López de. 1979. *Historia de la conquista de México*. Caracas: Biblioteca Ayacucho.

González Obregón, Luis, ed. 1910. *Proceso inquisitorial del cacique de Tetzcoco*. Publicaciones de la Comisión Reorganizadora del Archivo General y Público de la Nación 1. Mexico City: Secretaría de Relaciones Exteriores.

Gruzinski, Serge. 1988. *La colonisation de l'imaginaire: Sociétés indigènes et occidentalisation dans le Mexique espagnol; XVIe–XVIIIe siècle*. Paris: Gallimard. Translated as *The Conquest of Mexico: The Incorporation of Indian Societies into the Western World, Sixteenth–Eighteenth Centuries* (Cambridge: Polity Press, 1993).

Hassig, Ross. 2001. *Time, History, and Belief in Aztec and Colonial Mexico*. Austin: University of Texas Press.

———. 2006. *Mexico and the Spanish Conquest*. Norman: University of Oklahoma Press.

Herrera y Tordesillas, Antonio de. 1726–30. *Historia general de los hechos de los castellanos en las islas y tierra-firme del mar océano*. 4 vols. Madrid: Imprenta Real. (Orig. pub. 1601–4.)

Hicks, Frederic. 1994. "Texcoco, 1515–1519: The Ixtlilxochitl Affair." In *Chipping Away on Earth: Studies in Prehispanic and Colonial Mexico in Honor of Arthur J. O. Anderson and Charles E. Dibble,* edited by Eloise Quiñones Keber, 235–39. Lancaster, Calif.: Labyrinthos.

Horn, Rebecca. 1997. *Postconquest Coyoacan: Nahua-Spanish Relations in Central Mexico, 1519–1650.* Stanford: Stanford University Press.

Jones, Grant D. 1998. *The Conquest of the Last Maya Kingdom.* Stanford: Stanford University Press.

Kauffman, Leisa. 2014. "Alva Ixtlilxochitl's Colonial Mexican Trickster Tale: Nezahualcoyotl and Tezcatlipoca in the *Historia de la nación chichimeca.*" *Colonial Latin American Review* 23 (1): 70–83.

Kellogg, Susan. 1995. *Law and the Transformation of Aztec Culture, 1500–1700.* Norman: University of Oklahoma Press.

Kranz, Travis Barton. 2010. "Visual Persuasion: Sixteenth-Century Tlaxcalan Pictorials in Response to the Conquest of Mexico." In Schroeder 2010b, 41–73.

Lee, Jongsoo. 2008. *The Allure of Nezahualcoyotl: Pre-Hispanic History, Religion, and Nahua Poetics.* Albuquerque: University of New Mexico Press.

Lee, Jongsoo, and Galen Brokaw, eds. 2014. *Texcoco: Prehispanic and Colonial Perspectives.* Boulder: University Press of Colorado.

Leibsohn, Dana. 2009. *Script and Glyph: Pre-Hispanic History, Colonial Bookmaking, and the Historia Tolteca-Chichimeca.* Washington, D.C.: Dumbarton Oaks Research Library and Collection.

León-Portilla, Miguel. 1956. *La filosofía náhuatl estudiada en sus fuentes.* Mexico City: Ediciones Especiales del Instituto Indigenista Interamericano.

———. 1959. *Visión de los vencidos: Relaciones indígenas de la conquista.* With texts translated by Ángel María Garibay K. Mexico City: Biblioteca del Estudiante Universitario, Universidad Nacional Autónoma de México.

———. 1962. *The Broken Spears: The Aztec Account of the Conquest of Mexico.* Boston: Beacon Press.

———. 1979. "New Light on the Sources of Torquemada's *Monarchia indiana.*" *Americas* 35 (3): 287–316.

Lockhart, James. 1991. *Nahuas and Spaniards: Postconquest Central Mexican History and Philology.* Stanford: Stanford University Press.

———. 1992. *The Nahuas After the Conquest: A Social and Cultural History of the Indians of Central Mexico, Sixteenth Through Eighteenth Centuries.* Stanford: Stanford University Press.

———. 1993. *We People Here: Nahuatl Accounts of the Conquest of Mexico.* Berkeley: University of California Press.

———. 2001. *Nahuatl as Written: Lessons in Older Written Nahuatl, with Copious Examples and Texts.* Stanford: Stanford University Press.

Lockhart, James, and Stuart B. Schwartz. 1983. *Early Latin America: A History of Colonial Spanish America and Brazil.* Cambridge: Cambridge University Press.

Lovell, W. George, Christopher Lutz, Wendy Kramer, and William R. Swezey. 2013. *Strange Lands and Different Peoples: Spaniards and Indians in Colonial Guatemala*. Norman: University of Oklahoma Press.

Martínez, José Luis. 1982. *El "Códice Florentino" y la "Historia General" de Sahagún*. Mexico City: Archivo General de la Nación.

———. 1987. "Las Hibueras, despeñadero de desgracias." *Jahrbuch für Geschichte Lateinamerikas/Anuario de Historia de América Latina* 24:111–34.

———. 1990. *Hernán Cortés*. Mexico City: Universidad Nacional Autónoma de México.

Matthew, Laura E. 2012. *Memories of Conquest: Becoming Mexicano in Colonial Guatemala*. Chapel Hill: University of North Carolina Press.

Matthew, Laura, and Michel Oudijk, eds. 2007. *Indian Conquistadors: Indigenous Allies in the Conquest of Mesoamerica*. Norman: University of Oklahoma Press.

McEnroe, Sean F. 2014. *From Colony to Nationhood in Mexico: Laying the Foundations, 1560–1840*. Cambridge: Cambridge University Press.

Merrim, Stephanie. 1996. "The First Fifty Years of Hispanic New World Historiography: The Caribbean, Mexico, and Central America." In *The Cambridge History of Latin American Literature*, vol. 1, edited by Roberto González Echevarría and Enrique Pupo-Walker, 58–100. Cambridge: Cambridge University Press.

Mundy, Barbara E. 1996. *The Mapping of New Spain: Indigenous Cartography and the Maps of the "Relaciones Geográficas."* Chicago: University of Chicago Press.

Muñoz Camargo, Diego. 1986. *Historia de Tlaxcala*. Madrid: Historia 16.

Oudijk, Michel R. 2000. *Historiography of the Bènizàa: The Postclassic and Early Colonial Periods (1000–1600 A.D.)*. Leiden: CNWS.

Pastor Bodmer, Beatriz. 1992. *The Armature of Conquest: Spanish Accounts of the Discovery of America, 1492–1589*. Stanford: Stanford University Press.

Peterson, Jeanette Favrot. 1993. *The Paradise Garden Murals of Malinalco: Utopia and Empire in Sixteenth-Century Mexico*. Austin: University of Texas Press.

Phelan, John Leddy. 1970. *The Millennial Kingdom of the Franciscans in the New World*. 2nd ed. Berkeley: University of California Press.

Porras Muñoz, Guillermo. 1978. "Un golpe de estado contra Hernán Cortés." *Humanitas* 19:361–82.

Prescott, William H. 1843. *History of the Conquest of Mexico*. New York: Harper.

Restall, Matthew. 1997. *The Maya World: Yucatec Culture and Society, 1550–1850*. Stanford: Stanford University Press.

———. 1998. *Maya Conquistador*. Boston: Beacon Press.

———. 2003a. "A History of the New Philology and the New Philology in History." *Latin American Research Review* 38 (1): 113–34.

————. 2003b. *Seven Myths of the Spanish Conquest*. New York: Oxford University Press.

————. 2012. "The New Conquest History." *History Compass* 10 (2): 151–60.

Restall, Matthew, and Florine Asselbergs. 2007. *Invading Guatemala: Spanish, Nahua, and Maya Accounts of the Conquest Wars*. Latin American Originals 2. University Park: Pennsylvania State University Press.

Restall, Matthew, and Felipe Fernández-Armesto. 2012. *The Conquistadors: A Very Short Introduction*. Oxford: Oxford University Press.

Ricard, Robert. 1966. *The Spiritual Conquest of Mexico: An Essay on the Apostolate and the Evangelizing Methods of the Mendicant Orders in New Spain, 1523–1572*. Berkeley: University of California Press.

Roa-de-la-Carrera, Cristián A. 2005. *Histories of Infamy: Francisco López de Gómara and the Ethics of Spanish Imperialism*. Boulder: University Press of Colorado.

Scholes, Frances V., and Ralph L. Roys. 1968. *The Maya Chontal Indians of Acalan-Tixchel: A Contribution to the History and Ethnography of the Yucatan Peninsula*. Norman: University of Oklahoma Press.

Schroeder, Susan. 1994. "Father José María Luis Mora, Liberalism, and the British and Foreign Bible Society in Nineteenth-Century Mexico." *Americas* 50 (3): 377–97.

————. 2007. "Introduction: The Genre of Conquest Studies." In Matthew and Oudijk 2007, 5–27.

————. 2010a. "Chimalpahin Rewrites the Conquest: Yet Another Epic History?" In Schroeder 2010b, 101–23.

————, ed. 2010b. *The Conquest All Over Again: Nahuas and Zapotecs Thinking, Writing, and Painting Spanish Colonialism*. Portland, Ore.: Sussex Academic Press.

Schroeder, Susan, Anne J. Cruz, Cristián Roa-de-la-Carrera, and David E. Tavárez, eds. and trans. 2010. *Chimalpahin's Conquest: A Nahua Historian's Rewriting of Francisco López de Gómara's "La conquista de México."* Stanford: Stanford University Press.

Schwaller, John F. 2014. "The Brothers Fernando de Alva Ixtlilxochitl and Bartolomé de Alva: Two 'Native' Intellectuals of Seventeenth-Century Mexico." In *Indigenous Intellectuals: Knowledge, Power, and Colonial Culture in Mexico and the Andes*, edited by Gabriela Ramos and Yanna Yannakakis, 39–59. Durham: Duke University Press.

Schwaller, John F., and Helen Nader. 2014. *The First Letter from New Spain: The Lost Petition of Cortés and His Company, June 20, 1519*. Austin: University of Texas Press.

Sell, Barry D., Louise M. Burkhart, and Elizabeth R. Wright. 2008. *Nahuatl Theater*. Vol. 3, *Spanish Golden Age Drama in Mexican Translation*. Norman: University of Oklahoma Press.

Sousa, Lisa, and Kevin Terraciano. 2003. "The 'Original Conquest' of Oaxaca: Spanish and Mixtec Accounts of the Spanish Conquest." *Ethnohistory* 50 (2): 349–400.

Tavárez, David. 2011. *The Invisible War: Indigenous Devotions, Discipline, and Dissent in Colonial Mexico.* Stanford: Stanford University Press.

Taylor, William. 1972. *Landlord and Peasant in Colonial Oaxaca.* Stanford: Stanford University Press.

Terraciano, Kevin. 2001. *The Mixtecs of Colonial Oaxaca: Ñudzahui History, Sixteenth Through Eighteenth Centuries.* Stanford: Stanford University Press.

———. 2010. "Three Texts in One: Book XII of the Florentine Codex." *Ethnohistory* 57 (1): 51–72.

Torquemada, Juan de. 1943. *Monarquía indiana.* 3 vols. Mexico City: Chávez Hayhoe. (Orig. pub. 1723.)

Townsend, Camilla. 2014a. "Introduction: The Evolution of Alva Ixtlilxochitl's Scholarly Life." *Colonial Latin American Review* 23 (1): 1–17.

———. 2014b. "Polygyny and the Divided Altepetl: The Tetzcocan Key to Preconquest Politics Among the Nahuas." In Lee and Brokaw 2014, 93–116.

Velazco, Salvador. 2003. *Visiones de Anáhuac: Reconstrucciones historiográfícas y etnicidades emergentes en el México colonial; Fernando de Alva Ixtlilxóchitl, Diego Muñoz Camargo y Hernando Alvarado Tezozómoc.* Guadalajara: Universidad de Guadalajara.

Villella, Peter B. 2014. "The Last Acolhua: Alva Ixtlilxochitl and Elite Native Historiography in Early New Spain." *Colonial Latin American Review* 23 (1): 18–36.

Warren, J. Benedict. 1985. *The Conquest of Michoacán: The Spanish Domination of the Tarascan Kingdom in Western Mexico, 1521–1530.* Norman: University of Oklahoma Press.

Wolf, Gerhard, and Joseph Connors, eds. 2012. *Colors Between Two Worlds: The Florentine Codex of Bernardino de Sahagún.* Cambridge, Mass.: Harvard University Center for Italian Renaissance Studies.

Wood, Stephanie Gail. 2003. *Transcending Conquest: Nahua Views of Spanish Colonial Mexico.* Norman: University of Oklahoma Press.

Yannakakis, Yanna. 2011. "Allies or Servants? The Journey of Indian Conquistadors in the *Lienzo of Analco.*" *Ethnohistory* 58 (4): 653–82.

INDEX

Page references followed by *fig* indicate maps and illustrations.

Acalan province, 86, 86n92, 87, 88, 89
Acapichtlan, 33
Aculhuacan region, 28n36
Aculhua people
    Ahuaxpitzactzin as lord of, 31
    as allies of Spaniards, 28, 35, 39, 59
    in battle of Chalco, 32–33
    in battle of Mexico, 44, 45, 53
    in battle of Xochimilco, 35
    casualties of, 36, 65
    character of, 45
    expedition against kingdom of Pánuco, 67, 69
    expedition against Mixhuacan, 62
    expedition in provinces of Tetzcoco, 63, 64
    expedition to Honduras, 81, 83, 97, 100, 101, 106
    kinship with Mexica people, 45
    reputation as good warriors, 97
    as vassals of Ixtlilxochitl, 34n44, 36
Ahuatecpan, 86, 87
Ahuaxpitzactzin (Ahuaxpictzactzin), 31, 38–39, 44, 77
Ahuitzotl, ruler of Mexico-Tenochtitlan, 26n30
Albornoz, Rodrigo de, 81n83, 82
Almíndez Chirino, Pedro de Úbeda, 82, 83, 83n88
Altamirano, Diego, 106
Alva, Bartolomé de, 12n27
Alva Ixtlilxochitl, don Fernando de
    bias of accounts of, 91n96, 111
    career of, 14
    family of, 12–13, 12n27, 12n30

Historia de la nación chichimeca, 14n33
    as historian, 2
    historical sources used by, 19n3, 23n21, 44, 84, 108
    legacy of, 14
    perspectives on conquest of Mexico, 6, 14n33, 17
    spelling of proper names by, 19n4
    "Thirteenth Relation," 4
    on Topiltzin, 107n117
    use of Gómara's narrative by, 11–12, 95n104
    on vassals of Ixtlilxochitl, 31n41
    works of, 4n6, 20n9
Alvarado, Jorge de, 49
Alvarado, Pedro de
    conquest of Tototepec by, 64
    cruelty of, 48
    as deputy of Cortés, 24
    expedition in Guatemala, 70, 71, 72, 73, 74
    as godfather of Cohuanacoch, 76
    injury of, 73
    massacre of Mexica nobility, 25–26
    routes of military expeditions of, 61*fig*
    at siege of Mexico City, 42, 48–49, 51, 55
    at Tlacopan, 37, 39, 42
Amoan, 99
Anaxaxucan, town of, 85
Apoxpalon, ruler of Acalan, 88–89, 93–94, 95
Ascensión, Bay of, 86
Athelechuan, 73
Axayaca, don Alonso
    on death of King Cacama, 26
    on death of Tecocoltzin, 44

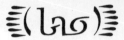

latin american originals

Titles in Print